THE ESSENTIALS OF MASSACHUSETTS MENTAL HEALTH LAW

A STRAIGHTFORWARD GUIDE FOR CLINICIANS OF ALL DISCIPLINES

THE ESSENTIALS OF MASSACHUSETTS MENTAL HEALTH LAW

A STRAIGHTFORWARD GUIDE FOR CLINICIANS OF ALL DISCIPLINES

STEPHEN H. BEHNKE, J.D., PH.D.
JAMES T. HILLIARD, J.D.

W. W. NORTON & COMPANY • NEW YORK • LONDON

For information about permission to reproduce selections
from this book, write to
Permissions, W. W. Norton & Company, Inc., 500 Fifth Avenue,
New York, NY 10110.

Library of Congress Cataloging-in-Publication Data

Behnke, Stephen H., 1958–
    The essentials of Massachusetts mental health law : a straightforward guide
    for clinicians of all disciplines / Stephen H. Behnke, James T. Hilliard.
        p. cm.
    "A Norton professional book."
    Includes bibliographical references and index.
    ISBN 0-393-70249-9
    1. Mental health laws—Massachusetts. I. Hilliard, James T. II. Title.
    KFM3765.B44 1998
    344.744'044—dc21   97-32855 CIP

W. W. Norton & Company, Inc., 500 Fifth Avenue, New York, N.Y. 10110
                    http://www.wwnorton.com
    W. W. Norton & Company Ltd., 10 Coptic Street, London WC1A 1PU
                    5 6 7 8 9 0

For My Parents

Sicut qui thesaurizat, ita et qui honorificat matrem suam, qui honorat patrem suam iucundabitur in filiis et in die orationis suae exaudietur. (From the Book of Sirach, on the Feast of the Holy Family)

—S.H.B.

To My Mother and Father

Thanks for bringing me up the right way.

—J.T.H.

CONTENTS

ACKNOWLEDGMENTS

I am deeply grateful to the following individuals and groups for so generously offering their help, encouragement, and support in the preparation of this book: Bob Goisman, for first providing me a forum to teach and discuss the material in this book, and for his continued interest in and support of my work; Adam Bemporad, for legal research; Shirlene Sampson, for eagerly suggesting questions relevant to clinical work; Pat Fernandez, for her thoughtful insights and comments on the family law section; Jim Preis, for his critique of the book's introduction to the law; members of the Massachusetts Mental Health Center's Program in Psychiatry and the Law, for their *unbelievably* direct comments on the informed consent letter; Kitty Howard, for her thoughtful and patient leadership of the Massachusetts Mental Health Center's Executive Office, and for her generosity in answering the many questions Center clinicians bring to her each day; Margaret Henehan, for her careful review of the section on civil commitment; Scott Monahan, for his legal research and his comments on the chapter concerning professional liability; Ken Duckworth, for his continued efforts to address the stigma attached to mental illness; Don Meyer, for sharing his expertise on the supervisor-supervisee relationship; Phil Salhaney, for his support in my writing this book and his willingness to read multiple drafts of numerous sections; Seth Rafal, for his continued interest in exploring how to integrate concerns about risk management with excellent clinical care; Tony Kalinowski, for his ongoing eagerness to discuss the ethical dimensions of working with Massachusetts Mental Health Center clients; the Massachusetts Mental Health Center's Department of Psychology, for their kindness and support of my work; Robert Mendoza, for his enormously insightful comments on earlier drafts of this book, as well as for taking on the considerable task of simply being Robert Mendoza; Eunice Lucas, for encouraging me to keep writing; and Patti LeBlanc, for the gentle manner in which she provided her help and attention during all the many months the manuscript was being written.

I would like to thank Ralph Engle, Thomas Gutheil, Jay Patel, Hudie Siegel, Justin Weiss, and June Wolf. Each of these truly extraordinary individuals has shown me kindness and support in ways that extend far beyond this book. I hope that my work will serve as a tribute to their mentorship, and I am deeply grateful for having had the opportunity to know them.

I would like to thank my coauthor, Jim Hilliard. Without doubt, the best part of writing this book was working with Jim. His thoughtful, studied, and kind manner has come to represent for me the very best in what the law has to offer and I hope that, one day, people will speak about me in the same manner they speak about Jim today.

Finally, I would like to thank Jonathan Defelice, Kunya Des Jardins, and Elyn Saks, whose warmth, understanding, and friendship has meant more to me than I could express in words.

—Stephen H. Behnke

I wish to acknowledge Dr. Stephen Behnke, whose persistence and hard work made this book possible; my secretary, Patti LeBlanc, who kept me organized; and my wife, Linda, whose confidence and support were invaluable.

—James T. Hilliard

INTRODUCTION

The idea for this book arose from our teaching at the Massachusetts Mental Health Center and Harvard Medical School and our consulting to mental health professionals about problems in risk management. The most frequent comment from trainees and experienced clinicians alike—that it is enormously helpful to have laws relevant to clinical practice explained in a simple and straightforward way—suggested the need for a book to orient mental health professionals to their legal rights and responsibilities.

The purpose of this book is to set forth, in a clear and concise manner, the laws most relevant to mental health practice in the Commonwealth of Massachusetts. The book is also designed to explain and demonstrate how these laws apply to the many problems mental health professionals encounter on a day-to-day basis. The format will be useful both to the student trainee and to the more senior clinician; indeed, the majority of treaters find it difficult to keep up to date on how the Massachusetts legislature and courts have changed the legal landscape of clinical practice. Lawyers, as well, may find the explanations of state laws governing mental health practice useful to their understanding of this interesting and ever-changing field.

The Essentials of Massachusetts Mental Health Law is divided into two parts. The three chapters of part I serve as a general introduction to the law. The first chapter, A Brief Introduction to the Law, explains where the different laws affecting clinical practice come from and, should a treater feel particularly bold, how she would go about finding an actual statute, court decision, or regulation.

The second chapter, *Tarasoff* and its Massachusetts Progeny, takes an actual statute and illustrates how a law "works." This chapter sets forth the philosophy of the Massachusetts *Tarasoff* law, explains what the law requires, what consequences follow when the requirements are not met, and what protections are afforded when they are, and demonstrates how different parts of the law fit together like building blocks to form a coherent whole. *Tarasoff* and its Massachusetts Progeny explains *why* the law was written, *what* the law says, and *how* the law goes about saying it. Any law can be analyzed in this manner, as we hope will become clear throughout the book.

The third and final chapter in part I discusses the set of laws and regulations perhaps most central to actual practice, those that pertain to privacy, confidentiality, and testimonial privilege. *Privacy* is an individual's right to make important life decisions—what to wear, whether to have children, which profession to pursue—without interference from the government. *Confidentiality* is the right to have communications with a therapist kept solely between the therapist and patient. *Testimonial privilege,* often referred to simply as *privilege,* is the patient's right to prevent a therapist from divulging confidential information in a legal proceeding. Chapter 3 includes a discussion of mandatory reporting laws; these laws require a mental health professional to break confidentiality when certain circumstances are present. The actual texts of the confidentiality, privilege, and mandatory reporting laws are found in appendix A. By the end of part I the reader should have a good sense of how a law can be read, understood, and applied in clinical practice.

Part II consists of 150 questions clinicians often ask about Massachusetts mental health law. We have divided the questions into ten topic headings. Topics range from the standard for committing an individual to a psychiatric hospital, to the rules of confidentiality that govern consultations, to the legal implications of serving as a therapist's "med backup," to the wisdom of meeting with a family after a patient commits suicide. Answers to these questions describe in a clear, direct manner how the law affects clinical practice. In appendix B are several examples of written materials that clinicians may find helpful at some point in their practice. These materials include an informed consent letter to begin a psychotherapy, a letter terminating a therapy with a difficult patient, and a reply to a board of registration letter of complaint. A sample subpoena is also included.

At the heart of this book is our belief that good patient care and knowledge of the law go hand-in-hand. Our experience is that, far from restricting or inhibiting clinical practice, knowing the essentials of

Massachusetts mental health law will free treaters from much undue—and unwarranted—anxiety about their legal rights and duties. We hope that such freedom will allow clinicians to concentrate on what they do best and enjoy most—treat patients.*

---

* A brief word about terminology. Solely for ease of reading, "client" and "patient" are used interchangeably, as are "clinician," "treater," "therapist," and "mental health professional." By "client" and "patient" we mean any individual who seeks services from a mental health professional. By the latter four terms we mean any individual who provides such services.

Part I

An Introduction to the Law

1

A Brief Introduction to the Law

The American system of law is divided into two layers: federal and state. Federal laws affect the United States as a whole, while state laws are specific to a particular state or commonwealth. As a citizen of Massachusetts, you are a citizen of the Commonwealth and a citizen of the United States. You are thus accorded the rights and privileges, as well as the responsibilities, afforded by both federal and state law. While our discussion will focus primarily on laws made in the Commonwealth, we will also mention important federal laws that affect the good citizens of Massachusetts.

The laws of the Commonwealth may be similar to laws found in other states, but always keep in mind that any state law is binding only for that state. Because each state is its own sovereignty, each is free to decide for itself what laws to enact, which means that things can get a bit confusing, since the 50 states may have 50 different laws governing the same topic. What's important is to keep in mind whether a law is a *state* law; if so, then, should you reside in that same state, the law applies to you and you are bound to follow it. If the law belongs to another state, then it is not binding on you, although you will want to know what your state says about the particular topic.

Our discussion will address, and explain how to cite, four types of laws: (1) the constitution; (2) statutes enacted by the legislature; (3) regulations promulgated by administrative agencies; and (4) decisions made by courts. Although the hierarchical relationships between the Constitution, statutes, regulations, and court decisions can become quite complicated, each of these four is nevertheless considered part of the law.

An outline of the discussion on how to cite Massachusetts laws is found on page 7.

The first and most important law in the Commonwealth and in the federal government is the Constitution. A constitution is that document whose provisions are sometimes referred to as "supreme," because no law can be enacted that conflicts with anything the constitution says. Many times a constitution will have a preamble that invokes its philosophical or moral basis. The Constitution of the United States, for example, begins, "We the people . . ." and thus makes clear that its moral basis is found in the assent of the people of the United States. The Commonwealth's Constitution, upon which the United States Constitution is based, starts off, "The end of the institution, maintenance, and administration of government, is to secure the existence of the body politic . . ." thus conveying that the continued existence and well-being of its citizenry is the Massachusetts Constitution's raison d'être. Simply put, a constitution is the touchstone by which a law will be deemed legitimate or illegitimate, and this is why our starting point for discussing law begins with recognizing the importance, indeed supremacy, of the Constitution.

The second category of laws are rules written by the legislature. These laws, referred to as "statutes," are written by the senators and representatives whom we elect. The senators and representatives meet in what is usually called the legislature, although people in the Bay State call it the "Massachusetts General Court." The United States Congress is the legislature for the federal government. The representatives gather, spend much time collecting information, even more time arguing with one another, and then write a bill which, if signed by the Governor or the President, becomes a law. A Massachusetts law is referred to by the initials "M.G.L.," which stand for *Massachusetts General Laws*. M.G.L. c.123, §36B, for example, refers to Massachusetts General Laws, chapter 123, section 36B.

The third group of laws is not written by the legislature at all and, in fact, these laws are not even called laws. These laws are called "regulations." Regulations are written by different groups of people, often those in charge of agencies, such as the Massachusetts Department of Mental Health and the Federal Food and Drug Administration. Regulations get their legitimacy through the legislature, which generally has neither the time nor the expertise to get into the nitty-gritty of running an administrative agency. It is as if the legislature were to say, "Look, we can provide the general contours of your work, but really know very little about what your agency does on a day-to-day basis. We therefore delegate to you the authority to run the agency, and to carry out your mission, in the way that makes most sense. You fill in the details about how things will get done." The details are the regulations written by the people who run the agency. Regulations must be consistent with the statutes they are designed to carry out. A Massachusetts regulation is referred to by the initials "CMR," which stand for *Code of Massachusetts Regulations*. 104 CMR 27.05, for example, refers to the Code of Massachusetts Regulations, chapter 104, section 27.05.

The fourth and final group of laws to discuss are those found in court decisions. Laws that arise from court decisions are referred to as "case law." Case law is what many people most associate with the law, even though, as we've seen, much law comes from elsewhere. In fact, technically speaking, no law should ever derive from the decision of a court, because the purpose of a court is to *interpret*, rather than to write, a law.

Case law is law that, in most instances relevant to our purposes, comes from a particular kind of court, an "appellate court." A court is an appellate court when it deals with cases "on appeal," that is, when someone doesn't like the decision of a lower court (usually a trial court) and so asks a higher court to review the lower court's decision. The holding of an appellate court is referred to as "law" because, like the Constitution, statutes, and regulations, the court's holding is legally binding; the court's holding is referred to as "case law" because it derives from a case. "Common law," a phrase you may have heard, is case law that has developed over a long, long time—many centuries, in fact.

In the Commonwealth of Massachusetts there are two appellate courts: the Massachusetts Appeals Court and the Supreme Judicial Court (referred to in shorthand as the SJC). The SJC, the highest court in the Commonwealth, is where one appeals a decision of the Massachusetts Appeals Court, although in certain circumstances a case can be appealed directly from a trial court to the SJC. In most instances, then, the SJC is "the appeals court to the appeals court." It is the highest of the three tiers in the Commonwealth's judicial system. Likewise, in the federal system there are federal appeals courts to which one may appeal the decision of a lower federal court. Above the federal appeals courts is the United States Supreme Court. The

United States Supreme Court is the highest federal court.

Massachusetts cases are cited in one of two ways: "Mass. App. Ct." is the abbreviation for cases from the Massachusetts Appeals Court; "Mass." is the abbreviation for cases of the Massachusetts Supreme Judicial Court (SJC). The numbers before and after the initials refer to the volume, page number, and date of the opinion. 263 Mass. 491 (1988), for example, means that this opinion was written by the SJC in 1988 and is found in volume 263, page 491 of the *Massachusetts Reports*, the series of volumes containing the opinions of the SJC.

The laws we have discussed—the constitutions, statutes, regulations, and case law—can all be found in law libraries, which are available to anyone who wishes to use them. Each county in the Commonwealth has a trial court with its own library, and the Commonwealth's law library is located in Boston. You should feel free to browse to your heart's content. If you'd like to find a law, simply go to the reference librarians, people who are more than happy—and sometimes literally ecstatic—to help you find what you're looking for.

Our discussion of laws is not complete without mention of professional codes of ethical conduct. Codes of ethics are not considered law. They are written by private associations and may be amended without the consent or approval of an elected representative, judge, or government employee. Nevertheless, codes of ethics do establish acceptable standards of conduct. State regulations may adopt a profession's code of ethics; as an example, the Code of Massachusetts Regulations (251 CMR 1.10) adopts the *Ethical Principles* of the American Psychological Association (1992) as the official guide for the Board of Registration of Psychologists. In addition, certain laws provide that a member of a profession can be sanctioned by a state regulatory body if he is found to have deviated from his profession's code of ethics. For this reason, it behooves a mental health professional to be intimately familiar with his or her profession's code of ethical conduct, and to think of that code as if it were law because, in a way, it is—it is the law of the profession.

One final comment. As comprehensive as our discussions will be, there are probably one or two things that we do not cover and that you'd learn if you spent $100,000 and three years in law school. Should you find yourself faced with a legal question, *consult a lawyer*. Cases involving law and mental health can be exceedingly complex and require legal expertise that no book, pamphlet, or review will provide. Educating yourself about the law by reading statutes and court decisions is an enormously worthwhile endeavor. Educating yourself about brain surgery is enormously worthwhile as well. But don't go after that tumor with your Swiss army knife.

LAWS AFFECTING MENTAL HEALTH PRACTICE

I.   Constitution
    A.   Supreme law of the land
    B.   No law may conflict with the Constitution.

II. Statutes
    A.   Written by the legislature
        1.   United States Congress for federal laws
        2.   Massachusetts General Court for Massachusetts laws
    B.   Massachusetts statutes referred to as, e.g., M.G.L. c.123, §36B
        (Massachusetts General Laws, chapter 123, section 36B)

III. Regulations
    A.   Written by agencies, with authority from the legislature
    B.   Massachusetts regulations referred to as, e.g., 104 CMR 27.05
        (Code of Massachusetts Regulations, chapter 104, section 27.05)

IV. Cases
    A.   Generally written by appellate courts
    B.   Massachusetts cases referred to as, e.g.:
        1.   413 Mass. 182 (1992)
        (1992 opinion of the Massachusetts Supreme Judicial Court [SJC], found in volume 413 of the Massachusetts Reports, at page 182)
        2.   16 Mass. App. Ct. 271 (1983)
        (1983 opinion of the Massachusetts Appeals Court, found in volume 16 of the Massachusetts Appeals Court Reports, at page 271)

V.   Codes of ethics
    A.   Written by professional associations
    B.   Establish standards of conduct for profession
    C.   May be brought into Massachusetts law by way of CMR (e.g., Code of Massachusetts Regulations adopts American Psychological Association's 1992 Code of Ethics)

2

TARASOFF AND ITS MASSACHUSETTS PROGENY

Most clinicians have heard the word "Tarasoff," usually uttered with some understandable, yet unfortunate, combination of anxiety and obligation. Of such magnitude is the aura surrounding *Tarasoff* that for many clinicians the very word has become synonymous with the concept of law and psychiatry. In reality, however, issues implicated by the *Tarasoff* case and its legal progeny account for a small percentage of forensic cases. Moreover, once the legal ruling is explained, much of the attendant anxiety usually disappears. Indeed, unbeknownst to many, *Tarasoff* entails a fascinating story.

Below is a discussion of the events that lead to the *Tarasoff* case and an analysis of the law that Massachusetts enacted as a response. Our discussion takes the Massachusetts law apart, then puts it back together again, to show how the various elements of this law form a coherent whole around a particular set of values. The relevance of this discussion is that often a situation will arise that has no clear corollary in the law—no case, statute, or regulation will address directly what you should *do*. In fact, our experience is that most situations fall into this category. When faced with such a situation, *the process by which a clinician decides what to do* becomes as important as the decision itself. The documentation of this process should show that the clinician appreciates what values are at stake, and should demonstrate a thoughtful application of those values to the matter at hand. This appreciation, thoughtful application of the values embodied in a mental health law, and documentation of the decision-making process will be a clinician's very best protection against liability.

THE LEGAL LANDSCAPE

To understand why the *Tarasoff* case has so captured the imagination of clinicians, one must examine two aspects of our legal system: first, how the law views affirmative duties (legal obligations) to third parties; and second, the concept of negligence. In terms of the former, the American legal system rarely imposes legal obligations unless two or more individuals have freely entered into a legal agreement that creates corresponding duties. In legal terms, one rarely owes a duty to third parties. Take as an example that one morning I decide to go for a walk on the pier next to where I live, and suddenly hear a cry for help. Should I see someone going under for the third time, there is no *legal* obligation that I do anything—I can simply keep on walking, without concern that I will be sued or charged with a crime.* Should there be a life preserver right beside me, a telephone for emergencies only feet away, I remain under no legal obligation whatsoever to act. I owe this third party no *duty*—he does not know me, I do not know him, and we have not entered into a relationship creating legal duties to one another. From the law's point of view, our legal destinies are utterly independent.

An exception to this rule occurs should I begin a rescue, perhaps by picking up the life preserver and swinging it backward as if to throw it. In that case I have an obligation to make a reasonable attempt to complete the rescue. The reason behind the exception is that my commencing a rescue may serve to discourage others from acting—hence, if I begin to act in this instance, I have an obligation to follow through. This exception notwithstanding, the overriding principle is that the law will not impose a duty to act unless and until the individuals have entered into some relationship recognized by law.

---

* This manner of behaving will not, however, get one nominated for many humanitarian awards.

A second important concept upon which the *Tarasoff* case is built is that of *negligence*. Negligence is a form of tort. Tort is the legal term for the sort of mistake that gives rise to lawsuits in civil, as opposed to criminal, courts. Malpractice is a form of negligence, and hence is a tort.

A malpractice lawsuit is often said to consist of the "four Ds," defined as the Dereliction of a Duty Directly causing Damages. Each of the four Ds is an essential element of a malpractice claim—if any one is missing, the lawsuit cannot succeed. You might think of the four Ds as the wheels on a car—if even one is gone, the car stays put. In the example above, should the individual in the water drown and his estate attempt to sue me, my defense will be that I had no duty toward him and so cannot be held liable for negligence. One of the wheels is missing, so the suit cannot go anywhere. Likewise, in cases where there is dereliction of a duty, yet no damages, a suit for malpractice fails. This makes intuitive sense—no matter how bad my mistake, if you suffer no harm, you should not be able to collect moneys from me. Similarly, if I am derelict in my duty, yet that dereliction does not directly cause your damages, a suit in negligence cannot prevail. Again, this makes sense. If I make a mistake, and you happen to suffer a harm, yet my mistake did not *cause* your harm, I should not be held responsible for compensating you.

In a malpractice case, the plaintiff—the person who claims to have been harmed and is consequently bringing the lawsuit—must demonstrate by a preponderance of evidence, or 51% (see part II, question 4), that each of the four Ds is present. Each D has its own complexities; the manner in which one calculates damages, for example, can be enormously intricate, as can be showing direct causation. Dereliction of duty, also called "breach of duty," is somewhat unique, insofar as the standard by which to judge whether one is derelict remains constant. For those in the medical profession, one must provide care that is *reasonable*; one need not provide the best, most expensive, or most up-to-date care available. One only need provide care that is reasonable. Should one provide care that falls below what is reasonable, one can be considered derelict in one's duty.

Defining the fourth D, that of duty, involves answering two questions. First, *what* is the duty I owe? That is to say, I must determine what precisely my legal obligation entails. Second, *to whom* do I owe this duty? Now that I know what I must do, to whose benefit must I do it? It was in answering these two questions that the *Tarasoff* case broke new ground.

THE FOUR "Ds" OF NEGLIGENCE

I. Dereliction: The mental health professional must provide care that is reasonable. If the care falls below what is reasonable, the mental health professional is derelict.

    No dereliction = The lawsuit for malpractice fails.

II. Duty: The mental health professional has a legal relationship with an individual that gives rise to a duty.
    A. What is the duty? (An important point in *Tarasoff*)
    B. To whom is the duty owed? (An important point in *Tarasoff*)

    No duty = The lawsuit for malpractice fails.

III. Directly causing: The dereliction of duty must directly cause the damages.

    No direct causation = The lawsuit for malpractice fails.

IV. Damages: The person bringing a negligence suit must have suffered harm.

    No damages = The lawsuit for malpractice fails.

THE FACTS OF THE CASE

Early in July of 1969 a young man named Prosenjit Poddar arrived at an appointment to see a clinician at the University of California, Berkeley, student health center. Poddar, a 25-year-old Bengalese Indian graduate student, had come to the student health center at the urging of a friend who had become concerned over Poddar's obsession with a 19-year-old undergraduate of Russian lineage, Tatianna Tarasoff. By the time Poddar arrived at the student health center that summer he had been transformed from a student with enormous potential and industriousness to a loner who spent hour upon hour in his room listening to secretly recorded audiotapes of his conversations with Tatianna. After meeting at a folk dance for international students nearly a year earlier, Poddar and Tatianna had shared a lingering flirtation but, to Poddar's great disappointment, no more.

Following his initial appointment at the student health center Poddar began treatment with a clinical psychologist, Dr. Lawrence Moore. Poddar told Dr. Moore that he was going to kill a girl whom he did not name, but who was identifiable as Tatianna. Shortly thereafter Poddar left therapy, almost certainly in response to Dr. Moore's statement that he would have to restrain Poddar should Poddar continue to talk of killing Tatianna. After consulting with colleagues, Dr. Moore wrote a letter to the Berkeley police, which read, in part:

> He is at this point a danger to the welfare of other people and himself. That is, he has been threatening to kill an unnamed girl who he feels has betrayed him and has violated his honor. He has told a friend . . . that he intends to go to San Francisco to buy a gun and that he plans to kill the girl. . . . Mr. Poddar should be committed for observation in a mental hospital. (Winslade & Ross, 1983)

The campus police found and questioned Poddar. After extracting from Poddar a promise to stay away from Tatianna, however, the police released him. The director of the department of psychiatry then ordered that Poddar not be committed to a psychiatric hospital. Neither the campus police nor anyone at the student health center warned Tatianna or her parents of Poddar's threat. A few weeks later, on October 27, Poddar went to Tatianna's home and killed her.

Tatianna's parents brought a lawsuit against a number of individuals at UC Berkeley, including Dr. Moore and his colleagues. Their claim was based upon an action in negligence: The treaters had been derelict in their duty to warn Tatianna of Poddar's threat, a dereliction that directly caused Tatianna's death. The therapists—now defendants in the lawsuit—responded that they had no relationship with Tatianna, and so had no duty toward her. In the absence of a duty, they reasoned, a lawsuit could not succeed. They argued that, in addition to owing no duty to Tatianna, therapist-patient confidentiality actually prohibited them from disclosing this information. The defendants argued that the case was open and shut: What happened to Tatianna was a tragedy but, with one of the four Ds (duty) missing and with the constraints of confidentiality, a tragedy that had no place being decided in a court of law.

The lawsuit had an extremely high profile because of its possible implications. If Tatianna Tarasoff's parents were to prevail, therapists could have a duty toward people with whom they had no professional relationship, perhaps whom they had never met nor even seen. While courts had held psychiatrists responsible for damage done when their patients were prematurely released from an inpatient psychiatric facility, this case was different: Poddar was an outpatient, and Dr. Moore was a psychologist, raising the specter that the ruling would encompass all mental health professionals, who could henceforth be held responsible for harms committed by *any* of their patients. The American Psychiatric Association judged the case to be of such import that it entered the fray as an *amicus curiae*, Latin for "friend of the court." An amicus curiae is an organization which, while neither a plaintiff nor a defendant, nevertheless has an interest in the outcome of a case. The APA, fearing that with the stroke of a pen the court might significantly increase the number of individuals who could sue a therapist and win, argued "that even when a therapist does in fact predict that a patient poses a serious danger of violence to others, the therapist should be absolved of any responsibility for failing to act to protect the potential victim" (*Tarasoff* at 345). Put in other words, the APA wanted a blanket rule that a therapist is not liable to third parties whom a patient injures, even if the therapist could predict that the patient would be violent.

The court's first order of business was to examine whether there was any sort of relationship between Dr. Moore and Tatianna that the law would recognize. Such a relationship would give rise to a duty, and so supply the missing "D." To address this question the court reviewed case law that held that a duty may arise when there is a "special relationship" between two individuals. A "special relationship," the court explained, could give rise to affirmative duties toward third persons in cases where a third person is the foreseeable victim of some harm. The court examined the doctor-patient relationship between Dr. Moore and Poddar, and concluded that it was indeed this sort of "special relationship."* Thus, the court reasoned, in virtue of Dr. Moore's "special relationship" to Poddar, Dr. Moore owed a duty to Tatianna Tarasoff, the foreseeable victim of Poddar's harm. Put another way, the court concluded *that Dr. Moore had a duty to Tatianna Tarasoff because she was the foreseeable victim of his patient's harm.* In less than two pages, the court had supplied the absent "D."

Having concluded that Dr. Moore and his colleagues did owe Tatianna a duty, the court's next order of business was to determine how that duty should be defined. Perhaps the greatest misunderstanding about the Tarasoff case is on precisely this point. The court stated,

---

* Part of the court's thinking may well have been that the "special" nature of the therapist-patient relationship makes it likely that a patient would tell a therapist about feelings of wanting to hurt someone.

[O]nce a therapist does in fact determine, or under applicable professional standards reasonably should have determined, that a patient poses a serious danger of violence to others, he bears a duty to exercise reasonable care *to protect* [italics added] the foreseeable victim of that danger. (345)

The *Tarasoff* case held that the duty a therapist owes to third parties is the duty *to protect*—not, as is commonly misunderstood, the duty *to warn*. The difference is far more than merely semantic. There are many ways to protect a potential victim that do not necessitate warning. At times, warning may even *increase* the likelihood that a victim will be harmed. Our discussion of the Massachusetts statute will examine how one state has offered alternatives to warning as ways of fulfilling the duty to protect spelled out in *Tarasoff*.

The court was then presented with the question of how broad a circle of potential victims the duty to protect should encompass. Again the APA weighed in, arguing "that warnings must be given only in those cases in which the therapist knows the identity of the victim." The APA's approach could be characterized as, "Therapists should not be liable to third parties at all, but if the court decides they are, they should be liable only to those third parties who have been identified." The *Tarasoff* court was not so restrictive in its thinking. Addressing the question of whether a therapist must know exactly who the potential victim is before a duty arises, the court explained,

[I]n some cases it would be unreasonable to require the therapist to interrogate his patient to discover the victim's identity, or to conduct an independent investigation. But there may also be cases in which a moment's reflection will reveal the victim's identity. The matter thus is one which depends upon the circumstances of each case, and should not be governed by any hard and fast rule. (345)

The court left open the possibility that the duty to protect could extend to individuals whom the therapist had not yet identified, yet who could be known after "a moment's reflection." This seemingly innocuous comment has given rise to an enormous debate over the extent to which a therapist must know, or be able to determine, who the potential victim is before a duty to that third person arises. Some states, for example, require that the potential victim be identified before any duty arises. Other states have been far more expansive, creating a duty to protect when it becomes clear that anyone—regardless who—will be harmed. Below we will see how Massachusetts has dealt with this issue.

The *Tarasoff* case examined the second of the four Ds—duty—in a way that no court had done before. The court answered the two central questions about the duty owed by a therapist to a third party: The duty owed is the duty *to protect,* and the duty is owed to *foreseeable victims of harm who can be identified after "a moment's reflection."* The heart of the case, however, lies in how it directly pitted two values—confidentiality and public safety—against one another. There was no way to finagle. Given the way the court framed the issue, it had to choose one value at the expense of the other. The court came down decidedly in favor of public safety. In perhaps its most famous quotation, the *Tarasoff* court concluded,

> the public policy favoring protection of the confidential character of patient-psychotherapist communications must yield to the extent to which disclosure is essential to avert danger to others. *The protective privilege ends where the public peril begins* [italics added]. (347)

The balance struck by the court—that protective privilege must yield to public safety—is the foundation of the *Tarasoff* ruling. Before turning to see how the Commonwealth of Massachusetts has addressed the issues raised by the *Tarasoff* decision, we leave the reader with two historical notes on what happened to those most intimately involved with Tatianna's murder.

In the criminal matter, Poddar was charged with first degree murder. After a trial, at which much evidence concerning his mental status was heard, he was found guilty of second-degree murder and sent to a state prison. Poddar appealed and, five years later, the California Supreme Court overturned his conviction. The state was then in the position of putting Poddar on trial again for Tatianna's murder; instead, however, the prosecutor struck a bargain with Poddar's attorney. In exchange for not retrying the criminal case, Poddar's attorney would ensure that Poddar would return home and not come back to the United States. Today Poddar is married and living in India.

In the civil matter, the California Supreme Court announced its rule of law—that therapists have a duty to protect foreseeable victims of harm who can be identified after a moment's reflection—and instructed the trial court to apply this rule of law to determine whether Dr. Moore and his colleagues had been negligent in fulfilling their duty. Questions of fact before the trial court would therefore have been: Was Tatianna Tarasoff a foreseeable victim of Poddar's harm? If so, did Dr. Moore and his colleagues fulfill their duty to Tatianna by notifying the campus police? If notifying the police did *not* suffice to fulfill their duty, did their failure to take additional steps directly cause Tatianna's death? Before the case could make it back to the trial court, however, the parties reached a settlement—for a sum of money (which was never disclosed) Tatianna's parents agreed to go home and leave the courts behind. As a consequence, no clinician involved in Prosenjit Poddar's care was ever held liable for negligence in a court of law.

TARASOFF COMES TO MASSACHUSETTS

Tarasoff was decided by the California Supreme Court. Other states are free to follow its reasoning, or not, as they wish. Most states have enacted laws stipulating a duty to protect, but because each state is free to write its own law, the laws vary in important respects: How broad is the circle of potential victims encompassed by this duty? Must the victim be identified? Must the threat to a potential victim be explicit? Must the threat always consist of spoken words? Do spoken words threatening violence always give rise to a duty? What, in addition to a warning, does the duty to protect entail? The quality of a state law can be measured by how well it answers each of these questions, that is, by how well it guides therapists in knowing precisely what their legal obligations are. By this measure, Massachusetts has an excellent statute.

An outline of the essential elements of chapter 123, section 36B is found on page 22.

There are seven elements of this law that you should note. The first element concerns the individuals to whom the statute extends, any "licensed mental health professional." The definition of "licensed mental health professional" covers anyone who provides mental health services and who must obtain a license from the Commonwealth to do so. The definition is broad and extends to psychiatrists, psychologists, social workers, psychiatric nurses, sexual assault counselors, domestic violence victims' counselors, and "allied mental health and human service professionals," a category that includes marriage and family therapists, rehabilitation counselors, mental health counselors, and educational and school psychologists. If in doubt, and your work requires a license from

THE MASSACHUSETTS *TARASOFF* STATUTE

M.G.L. c.123, §36B

(1) There shall be no duty owed by a licensed mental health professional to take reasonable precautions to warn or in any other way protect a potential victim or victims of said professional's patient, and no cause of action imposed against a licensed mental health professional for failure to warn or in any other way protect a potential victim or victims of such professional's patient unless: (a) the patient has communicated to the licensed mental health professional an explicit threat to kill or inflict serious bodily injury upon a reasonably identified victim or victims and the patient has the apparent intent and ability to carry out the threat, and the licensed mental health professional fails to take reasonable precautions as that term is defined in section one; or (b) the patient has a history of physical violence which is known to the licensed mental health professional and the licensed mental health professional has a reasonable basis to believe that there is a clear and present danger that the patient will attempt to kill or inflict serious bodily injury against a reasonably identified victim or victims and the licensed mental health professional fails to take reasonable precautions as that term is defined by said section one. Nothing in this paragraph shall be construed to require a mental health professional to take any action which, in the exercise of reasonable professional judgment, would endanger such mental health professional or increase the danger to potential victim or victims.

(2) Whenever a licensed mental health professional takes reasonable precautions, as that term is defined in section one of chapter one hundred and twenty-three, no cause of action by the patient shall lie against the licensed mental health professional for disclosure of otherwise confidential information.

the Commonwealth, best to consider yourself covered until you can determine otherwise.

The second element is the manner in which the statute begins, "There shall be *no* [italics added] duty owed by a licensed mental health professional to take reasonable precautions to warn or in any other way to protect . . . unless . . ." This manner of beginning emphasizes the restrictive nature of the statute—liability is limited to specific circumstances. The statute thus sends a clear message to courts: "We, the legislature, intend this statute to be restrictive, rather than expansive." Without this particular beginning, courts might be inclined to find liability over and above the situations spelled out in the text of the statute, something the legislature wished to discourage.

The third noteworthy element of the Massachusetts statute is found in clause *a*, which indicates the initial conditions under which a therapist has a duty to act. This clause is extremely specific and, as such, in keeping with the restrictive nature of the law as a whole. For a duty to arise under this clause, (1) the patient must have communicated a threat *to kill or inflict serious bodily injury*, (2) the threat must be *explicit*, (3) the victim or victims must be *reasonably identified*, (4) the patient must have the *intent* to carry out the threat, and (5) the patient must have the *ability* to carry out the threat. Only when all five conditions are met does the therapist have a duty to take reasonable precautions to protect or to warn a potential victim. Note how Massachusetts has addressed issues raised by the *Tarasoff* decision. In doing so it tells the therapist precisely what must occur before she must act: In the absence of an explicit threat to kill or seriously injure a reasonably identified victim, by a patient who intends to carry out the threat and has the ability to do so, this clause will not impose a duty.

The fourth noteworthy element is found in clause *b*, which indicates a second set of conditions under which the therapist has a duty to act. For a duty to arise under clause *b*, (1) the patient must have a *history of physical violence*, (2) the history must be *known* to the mental health professional,* (3) the mental health professional must have a *reasonable basis* to believe that (4) there is a *clear and present danger*, (5) the clear and present danger must be that the patient will attempt *to kill or inflict serious bodily injury*, and (6) the danger must be directed against a *reasonably identified victim*. In certain respects clause *b* will necessitate more clinical judgment than clause *a*, insofar as a duty may arise in the absence of an explicit threat. Nevertheless, the statute remains enormously specific; there must be a known history of physical violence and a clear and present danger of death or serious bodily injury against a reasonably identified victim.

Note how in writing clauses *a* and *b* the Massachusetts legislature has provided far more guidance about when to act than did the *Tarasoff* decision itself. The California Supreme Court's decision directed clinicians to act when the harm was "foreseeable"—helpful, but not overly so. Many a debate could be held about when a particular act of violence was "foreseeable." Massachusetts, by contrast, directs clinicians to act when there is an "explicit" threat to "kill or inflict serious bodily injury," or when a

---

* A word of caution—you cannot escape your duty under this clause by willfully staying ignorant of your patient's history.

patient with a "known history of physical violence" presents "a clear and present danger" of inflicting such an injury. The specificity found in the language of the Massachusetts statute narrows and defines the duty.

The specificity of the language notwithstanding, the statute leaves ample room for clinical judgment. In the first condition, for example, an explicit threat is *not* sufficient to create a duty. The threat must be from someone with both the intent and the ability to carry out the threat. Often patients will bring into their therapies fantasies of wishing to harm, or even kill, another individual. Such rage may be the focus of your work with a patient. Obviously, every time a patient expresses the wish to kill, a duty is not created; many clinicians would spend most of their time on the phone were this the case. Rather, the clinician's task is to determine when patients are likely to *act* on their fantasies. Only then does the duty arise, and it is by relying on your clinical judgment that you will determine when a patient is likely to move from fantasy to action. Likewise with the second clause—a duty arises not in virtue of a patient's history of violence, but when the clinician has a "reasonable basis to believe" that a patient with such a history creates a "clear and present danger" to another individual. A judgment that a clear and present danger has arisen may entail examining under what conditions your patient was violent in the past, his current mental status, and external factors serving to exacerbate or mitigate the likelihood that he will kill or seriously injure someone. What's important is that while the statute provides much helpful guidance, your clinical judgment will ultimately determine whether you must act. In moments of uncertainty, consult with a colleague or an attorney knowledgeable in mental health law. Be sure to document your consultation, as well as your reasons for following the particular course of action you choose to follow. *Every bit as important as what you do will be a careful documentation of your consultation(s) and of the process by which you come to decide how to respond.*

The fifth element is found in the final sentence of paragraph 1. Here the statute states that, any other requirement notwithstanding, the mental health professional does not have a duty to act in any way that would either endanger herself or increase the danger to the potential victim. This is a crucial aspect of the statute—a clinician never need place herself in harm's way, and no duty will arise if a given course of action would *increase* the likelihood that a victim will be injured. As an example, a clinician would never attempt physically to restrain a patient, even if the situation fell unambiguously within clause *a* or *b*. The legislature has taken a very common sense approach, an approach that follows the philosophy set forth in *Tarasoff.* The foundation upon which *Tarasoff* was built lies in the court's statement that public safety trumps confidentiality—when safety is at issue, the privacy of the therapeutic relationship must give way. This equation makes safety paramount. It would therefore make little sense to encourage or require any course of action that would *increase* the likelihood of danger, thus subordinating safety to some other end. The statute is consistent both with itself and with *Tarasoff*—the purpose of acting will be to further public safety. When acting will endanger public safety, no duty to act arises.

The sixth element follows immediately upon the fifth and is likewise consistent both with the statute as a whole and with the *Tarasoff* decision. In paragraph 2, the statute states that whenever a mental health professional takes reasonable precautions to protect or to warn a potential victim under the conditions it sets forth, the clinician cannot be held liable for disclosing confidential material. This element restates the balance struck in *Tarasoff*—confidentiality yields to matters of safety—and, as a corollary to this balance, releases clinicians from liability when they further safety at the expense of confidentiality.

The seventh element is referred to by, yet not explicitly found in, the text of the statute. Several times the statute refers to the conditions under which a clinician must take "reasonable precautions." When the conditions found in *a* or *b* are met, for example, the clinician must take reasonable precautions and may be held liable for not doing so. The statute itself, however, never states explicitly what it means by this enigmatic phrase—that is to say, the statute never says what precautions are reasonable either when a patient communicates an explicit threat or when a clear and present danger arises with a patient whose history of physical violence is known to the clinician. What precisely must the clinician do? How will the clinician know what precautions are reasonable? Could more than one precaution be considered reasonable?

The Massachusetts legislature has, once again, provided helpful guidance. A separate statute, M.G.L. chapter 123, section 1, sets forth four courses of action that can be considered "reasonable precautions": (1) communicating the threat to the potential victim; (2) notifying a law enforcement agency near where the patient or the victim lives; (3) arranging for the patient to be voluntarily hospitalized; and (4) taking the steps available to place the patient in a hospital involuntarily. The clinician, exercising reasonable judgment, will use one or a combination of these

DEFINITION OF "REASONABLE PRECAUTIONS"

M.G.L. c.123, §1

"Reasonable precautions," any licensed mental health professional shall be deemed to have taken reasonable precautions, as that term is used in section 36B, if such professional makes reasonable efforts to take one or more of the following actions as would be taken by a reasonably prudent member of his profession under the same or similar circumstances:

(a)   communicates a threat of death or serious bodily injury to the reasonably identified victim or victims;

(b)   notifies an appropriate law enforcement agency in the vicinity where the patient or any potential victim resides;

(c)   arranges for the patient to be hospitalized voluntarily;

(d)   takes appropriate steps, within the legal scope of practice of his profession, to initiate proceedings for involuntary hospitalization.

four to fulfill her duty to protect, arising when the conditions in clauses *a* or *b* are met. Here, in starkest form, do we see the distinction between the duty to protect and the duty to warn.

CONCLUSION

The Massachusetts *Tarasoff* statute is a well-written law. It is well-written because it gives clinicians explicit guidance about when a duty to act arises and it tells clinicians what actions are appropriate to fulfill their duty. The statute also states how values are to be ordered: safety trumps confidentiality. As well-written as this statute is, however, there are many situations that leave the clinician wondering whether a duty has arisen and, if so, what she should do. Take, for example, the HIV-positive patient who insists on having unsafe sex with an unsuspecting spouse. It is unclear how—or whether—the *Tarasoff* statute applies (see part II, question 131 for our assessment of this case). In most instances no statute, regulation, or case will completely address questions about a clinician's legal responsibility.

In circumstances that have no clear resolution, the process by which a clinician resolves the problem becomes crucial. The clinician's apprecia-

TARASOFF COMES TO MASSACHUSETTS

M.G.L. c.123, §36B

I. The duty to take reasonable precautions to protect or to warn potential victims extends to all licensed mental health practitioners:
   A. Psychiatrists
   B. Psychologists
   C. Social workers
   D. Psychiatric nurse clinical mental health specialists
   E. Allied mental health and human services professionals
      1. Marriage and family therapists
      2. Rehabilitation counselors
      3. Educational psychologists
      4. Mental health counselors
   F. Sexual assault counselors
   G. Domestic violence victims' counselors
   H. Any other individual who holds him- or herself "out to the general public as one providing mental health services" and who must obtain a license to do such work

II. Licensed mental health practitioners are under no duty to take reasonable precautions to protect or to warn except under the two conditions set forth in the statute.

III. The two conditions that establish a duty to take reasonable precautions are:
   A. An **explicit** threat **to kill or seriously injure** a **readily identified** victim, made by an individual with the **intent** and the **ability** to carry out the threat.
   B. The clinician has a **reasonable basis to believe** that an individual with a **known history of physical violence** presents a **clear and present danger** of **killing or inflicting serious bodily injury** on a **readily identified** victim.

IV. Reasonable precautions (M.G.L. c.123, §1) are:
   A. Communicating threat to potential victim
   B. Notifying appropriate law enforcement agency
   C. Arranging for voluntary hospitalization
   D. Arranging for involuntary hospitalization

V. Clinician need not act in any way that would increase danger to self or victim.

VI. Clinician will not be held liable for disclosing confidential information if acting in accordance with the provisions of the statute.

tion of what values are at stake and her thoughtful application of those values to the matter at hand are what will matter most. While this chapter has discussed the values behind M.G.L chapter 123, section 36B, its more significant point is that a clinician's greatest protection against liability is not found in a book of laws. Rather, what protects a clinician from liability is her capacity to see what values are relevant to a particular circumstance, apply those values in a thoughtful manner to a problem that may have no clear answer, and document how she has come to decide on a particular course of action.

Having examined the *Tarasoff* statute in detail, we now turn to a series of statutes and regulations central to mental health law, those governing privacy, confidentiality, and testimonial privilege. Our discussion of these laws forms the body of the following chapter; the actual texts of the laws are found in appendix A. As you read, notice both what the laws say and how they are put together. Your understanding of how these statutes and regulations embody a coherent set of values will be an invaluable resource when confronted with a dilemma in your own practice.

3

Privacy, Confidentiality, and Testimonial Privilege

Privacy, confidentiality, and testimonial privilege affect the day-to-day life of a clinician perhaps more than any other area of mental health law, yet they remain elusive concepts. We have a sense that each of these words captures something important, but also feel a general fuzziness about what they share with one another and, perhaps more important, what is unique to each. And so we begin with definitions.

DEFINITIONS

Privacy is a broad concept that does not have a single, specific meaning. Justice Brandeis, a famous Justice of the United States Supreme Court, once called the right to privacy "the right to be let alone—the most comprehensive of rights and the right most valued by civilized men."* Justice Brandeis's definition captures the passive side of privacy, that which involves a right not to have others, most especially the government, interfere with our lives. The right to refuse medical treatment is an example of our passive right to privacy. Other aspects of privacy are more active and

* *Olmstead v. United States*, 277 U.S. 438, at 478 (1928).

are perhaps best thought of as the right to determine the course of one's wishes, hopes, and dreams—the right to live according to one's own life plan. These more active dimensions of privacy include the right to decide how to educate one's children, the right to travel where one pleases, the right to decide upon a profession, the right of an individual to choose "what he eats, wears, or reads."* Privacy, in its passive and active forms, covers a wide range of rights from the beginning to the end of life.

Confidentiality is an aspect, or a subset, of privacy. Confidentiality in the clinical context is the right to have things that are communicated to a therapist during a therapy kept in confidence, that is, not revealed to individuals who are outside the professional relationship. We refer to individuals outside the professional relationship as "third parties." Put in terms of *rights*, confidentiality is the patient's right to have information communicated in the course of the professional relationship remain within the bounds of the professional relationship. Put in terms of *obligations*, confidentiality is the obligation incumbent upon a mental health professional to ensure that what a client communicates in the course of the professional relationship stays within the bounds of the professional relationship.

Testimonial privilege, often referred to simply as *privilege*, is a subset of confidentiality. Testimonial privilege is the right of a patient to prevent a mental health professional from disclosing confidential information in a legal proceeding. Think of a mental health professional climbing the steps of a courthouse, preparing to testify about his work with a particular client. Suddenly he says to himself, "Wait—simply that I am about to enter a courthouse does not allow me to disclose material that othewise would be confidential. I must first consider my client's testimonial privilege."

The right to privacy is based upon a value central to our society, that of *individual autonomy*. Confidentiality and privilege, as subsets of privacy, also flow from individual autonomy. Autonomy is prized as a value because, as a society, we believe that an individual should be free to direct the course of his own life, free from intrusion, constraints, or interference, at least to the degree that his choices do not unduly interfere with the choices other people wish to make. Confidentiality and privilege respect autonomy by protecting an individual's right to share whatever information he chooses, with whomever he chooses. Confidentiality and

* *Kent v. Dulles*, 357 U.S. 116, at 125–126 (1958).

privilege ensure that the individual, and the individual alone, may determine the nature, content, and destination of his communications.

Confidentiality and privilege serve another important purpose. Communication is the tool of a mental health professional's trade, the raw material of a clinician's work. Protecting the sanctity of a patient's communications provides a safe haven for the patient to share the most intimate aspects of her life experience. The promise of confidentiality and privilege is thus the foundation of a successful clinical relationship.

WHERE THE LAWS ARE FOUND

An outline of the laws pertaining to privacy, confidentiality, and testimonial privilege is found on page 29.

The right to *privacy* is found in the United States Constitution. While the word "privacy" is not mentioned in the actual text of the Constitution, the Supreme Court has said that a number of the Constitution's amendments have penumbras—a word whose Latin roots mean "almost a shadow"—under which the right to privacy falls. Think of the Constitution as a great oak tree with sturdy limbs, long branches, and wide leaves. While no limb, branch, or leaf is emblazoned with the actual word "privacy," it is the oak's shade that creates, covers, and protects our right to privacy. Thus, the Supreme Court has reasoned that the term "liberty" in the Fourteenth Amendment implies certain privacy rights, even though the word "privacy" is not found in that, or in any other specific clause.

Massachusetts also has a statute that creates a right to privacy for citizens of the Commonwealth. M.G.L. chapter 214, section 1B states, "A person shall have a right against unreasonable, substantial, or serious interference with his privacy." Citizens of the Commonwealth, therefore, have both a right to privacy under the United States Constitution as well as a statutory right to privacy provided for by the General Laws of the Commonwealth.

A variety of laws speak to *confidentiality*. Certain laws provide that a patient has a right to confidentiality, while other laws obligate mental health professionals to keep patient material confidential. Confidentiality laws thus set forth the *rights* of patients and the *responsibilities* of mental health professionals.

Laws setting forth the responsibilities of mental health professionals to safeguard patient confidentiality are found in court decisions, statutes, and regulations. In *Alberts v. Devine*, 395 Mass. 59 (1985), the Massachusetts Supreme Judicial Court (SJC) held "that a duty of confidentiality arises from the physician-patient relationship." While *Alberts* created a duty for psychiatrists, a series of statutes and regulations created this duty for other mental health professionals. These statutes explicitly name psychologists, social workers, sexual assault counselors, domestic violence victims' counselors, and "allied mental health and human services professionals," a category that includes marriage and family therapists, rehabilitation counselors, educational psychologists, and mental health counselors. The Department of Mental Health, as well as facilities and licensees of the DMH, are likewise obligated by both statute and regulation to keep patient material confidential.

Two statutes set forth the rights of patients to confidentiality. First, under M.G.L. chapter 214, section 1B, the Massachusetts right to privacy statute, a disclosure of confidential information can be considered a violation of a patient's right to privacy. Put another way, because confidentiality is a subset of privacy, a breach of confidentiality can be considered a violation of an individual's right to privacy. Second, M.G.L. chapter 111, section 70E, the "Patients' Bill of Rights," says that "every patient and resident of a facility shall have the right . . . to confidentiality of all records and communications . . ." Note that these two statutes *entitle* patients to confidentiality and privacy, whereas the laws referred to in the paragraph above (see outline on page 29) *obligate* mental health professionals to keep material confidential. Thus, even were a discipline not specifically mentioned in a statute which obligates confidentiality, any client working with a member of that discipline may nevertheless be entitled to confidentiality by these other two statutes.

Two statutes speak explicitly to the issue of *testimonial privilege*, a patient's right to prevent a mental health professional from disclosing confidential information in a legal proceeding. M.G.L. chapter 233, section 20B states that privilege applies to "psychotherapists," defined as psychiatrists, psychologists, and psychiatric nurse mental health clinical specialists. M.G.L. chapter 112, section 135B applies testimonial privilege to social workers. These two statutes are not the only statutes relevant to testimonial privilege; other disciplines have single statutes that speak to *both* confidentiality and testimonial privilege. Combining confidentiality and testimonial privilege into one statute makes a modicum of sense, insofar as testimonial privilege may be thought of as confidentiality in the context of a legal proceeding. Nevertheless, the Massachusetts legislature has decided that for psychotherapists and social workers, the issue of testimonial privilege merits its own statute.

There are three things to keep in mind about laws governing testimonial privilege. First, the law does not like privilege, for the simple reason that privilege keeps information out of the judicial process. To the extent that information is kept out of the judicial process, courts are less likely to discover the truth. For this reason, lawyers say that "privilege suppresses truth."

The second point to keep in mind about privilege flows naturally from the first: Courts do not like to create testimonial privileges. Courts much prefer to defer to the legislature in this regard. Privilege is therefore created by statute, and only when a statute specifically names a discipline should a mental health professional assume that testimonial privilege applies. That is to say, only when a statute explicitly names your discipline should you assume that your client may rely on privilege to prevent you from disclosing information in a legal proceeding. As an example of the restrictive nature of testimonial privilege, the two privilege statutes apply only to *licensed* social workers and *licensed* psychotherapists. Confidential communications shared with an unlicensed psychotherapist or an unlicensed social worker cannot be kept out of a legal proceeding by virtue of testimonial privilege.

The final and perhaps most important point is that privilege *belongs to the client.* Your client may choose to allow you to testify in a legal proceeding, in which case the client is said to "waive privilege." The right to waive privilege, however, is your client's prerogative, and hers alone. If your client decides to "invoke privilege," you may not testify or otherwise disclose information in a legal proceeding unless and until you are ordered by a court to do so. If you cannot reach your client, perhaps because she has moved away, you may invoke privilege on your client's behalf. That you will invoke privilege on your client's behalf emphasizes how privilege belongs to your client—without a court order, you may not testify or release records unless your client gives you permission to do so (see chapter 7, Subpoenas and Court Orders).

Having defined privacy, confidentiality, and testimonial privilege, and having seen that each flows from the value of individual autonomy, we now turn to a more detailed discussion of Massachusetts laws that govern communications between a client and a mental health professional.

Confidentiality is addressed in so many places that the law has a Byzantine feel to it—often circuitous, repetitive, and disconcertingly stilted,

PRIVACY, CONFIDENTIALITY, AND TESTIMONIAL PRIVILEGE

I. Privacy: The right to decide how to live one's own life
   A. Constitution of the United States (penumbras of amendments to the Constitution, none of which specifically names a right to privacy)
   B. M.G.L. c.214, §1B (Massachusetts right to privacy statute)

II. Confidentiality: The client's right to have communications kept within the bounds of the professional relationship
   A. Laws that *obligate* mental health professionals not to reveal confidential information include:
      1. Psychiatrists (*Alberts v. Devine*, 395 Mass. 59 [1985])
      2. Licensed psychologists (M.G.L. c.112, §129A; 251 CMR 1.11)
      3. Licensed social workers (M.G.L. c.112, §135A; 258 CMR 22.00)
      4. Allied mental health and human service professionals (M.G.L c.112, §172)
         a. Licensed marriage and family therapists
         b. Licensed rehabilitation counselors
         c. Licensed educational psychologists
         d. Licensed mental health counselors
      5. Sexual assault counselors (M.G.L. c.233, §20J)
      6. Domestic violence victims' counselors (M.G.L. c.233, §20K)
      7. Department of Mental Health (M.G.L. c.123, §36; 104 CMR 27.18) *(Includes facilities and licensees of the DMH)*
   B. Laws that *entitle* clients to confidentiality include:
      1. M.G.L. c.214, §1B (right to privacy)
      2. M.G.L. c.111, §70E (Patients' Bill of Rights)

III. Testimonial privilege (or simply privilege): The client's right to prevent the mental health professional from revealing confidential communications in a legal proceeding
   A. Psychotherapists (M.G.L. c.233, §20B)
      1. Licensed psychiatrists
      2. Licensed psychologists
      3. Licensed psychiatric nurse clinical mental health specialists
   B. Licensed social workers (M.G.L. c.112, §135B)
   C. A client is said to "waive privilege" when she allows a mental health professional to reveal communications in a legal proceeding.
   D. A client is said to "invoke privilege" when she does not allow a mental health professional to reveal communications in a legal proceeding.
   E. If the client is unavailable, the mental health professional may invoke privilege on the client's behalf.

confidentiality statutes may seem to the mental health professional a case study in why law libraries are places to avoid. We hope the next section will persuade you otherwise. Below we discuss three sets of statutes: those that address *confidentiality*, those that address *testimonial privilege*, and mandatory reporting statutes.

CONFIDENTIALITY LAWS

Confidentiality statutes explicitly name psychologists, social workers, sexual assault counselors, domestic violence victims' counselors, and allied mental health and human services professionals (marriage and family therapists, rehabilitation counselors, educational psychologists, and mental health counselors). While these are the only disciplines explicitly named by statute, most of the principles discussed below apply to *all* mental health professionals. We will note when a particular clause applies only to a specific discipline. We will comment upon five elements of the Massachusetts confidentiality statutes, and then discuss the exceptions to confidentiality.

Massachusetts confidentiality laws, M.G.L c.112, §§* 129A, 135A, and 172; c.123, §36; and c.233, §§20J and 20K are found in appendix A. You do not need to read the laws in order to understand the discussion; nevertheless, the more familiar you are with the actual texts, the richer and more comprehensible the discussion will be. At the very least, read those laws that apply to your discipline.

The first element worthy of note concerns the difference in structure among the confidentiality statutes. Note how the psychologist and social worker statutes are lengthier and spell out a number of exceptions. The domestic violence victim's counselor statute, on the other hand, is much briefer and more absolute in its language. Also, psychiatrists, psychologists, and social workers have statutes for confidentiality separate from their statutes for testimonial privilege; other disciplines combine confidentiality and privilege into one statute. The allied mental health and human service professionals statute (c.112, §172), for example, begins "Any communica-

---

* *A double section sign indicates that more than one section of a chapter is under discussion. In this instance, three sections from chapter 112—section 129A, section 135A, and section 172—are made reference to.*

tion between (these disciplines) . . . and a client shall be deemed to be *confidential.* Said *privilege* shall be subject to waiver . . ." [italics added]. Thus, for these latter four disciplines, a single statute addresses both confidentiality and testimonial privilege.

The second noteworthy element is that each of the statutes makes "communications" confidential. "Communications" may entail more than merely words. Acts may be communications, and so confidential, as well. Perhaps the best way to capture the spirit of the law is to say that what a patient communicates to you—in whatever manner—is confidential, when the communication is reasonably understood as conveyed to you in your capacity as a mental health professional during the course of a professional relationship.

The third element important to note is found in the psychologist and social work statutes. These statutes extend the duty of confidentiality to any "colleague," "agent," or "employee" of a psychologist or social worker, "whether professional, clerical, academic, or therapeutic." While this language is found in only two of the confidentiality statutes, all mental health professionals should consider themselves obligated to follow its rule. The meaning is simple: Any individual with whom you work, regardless of whether that person is a cotherapist for a group, a secretary who types your reports, or an office staff who shreds obsolete records, is bound by confidentiality in the same way and to the same extent you are bound. If you employ these individuals, it is *your* responsibility to ensure that they understand both the meaning and importance of confidentiality.

The fourth element worthy of note in the confidentiality statutes has to do with language which, while again found only in the psychologist and social work statutes, likewise applies to all mental health professionals. In the words of the psychologist statute, "At the initiation of the professional relationship the psychologist shall inform the patient of the . . . limitations to the confidentiality of their communications." This point is both important and complicated.

This point is important because, for both clinical and legal reasons, *you never want your client to be surprised when you disclose confidential information.* We consider this point so important that we have named it "The Law of No Surprises." Clinicians will sometimes disclose information, with the intention of telling the client at some later point, when the issue comes up. A very bad idea. You should be up front and honest with your client whenever the necessity of disclosing information arises. Such honesty will be greatly enhanced if, as the statute exhorts, you inform your client at the outset that there may be situations in which the two of you decide or safety requires that information will be disclosed. Such an explanation at the beginning of your work will lay the groundwork should the need to disclose confidential information arise, and will not leave your client feeling as if you were working behind her back. *The four words you never want a client to begin a sentence with are: "You didn't tell me . . ."*

The Law of No Surprises is complicated because, despite the absolute language of the statute, you do not want to spend your entire first session reviewing in painstaking detail each and every circumstance in which you may have to break confidentiality. Such a contingency is neither clinically nor legally indicated. Your aim should be to address the topic in a way that speaks to your particular client. For example, if your client has a history of serious suicide attempts or a history of violence, you will want to emphasize the necessity of disclosing information should you feel that safety is at issue. Your phrasing may be something like, "Safety is our bottom line, so should there come a time when I feel safety—yours or anyone else's—is at issue, I may need to share some of the things we've talked about. If that happens, I'll make every effort to talk it over with you first and, if at all possible, we'll share the information together."

This communication creates a frame for your work by conveying that safety is the foundation upon which the treatment rests. The communication also conveys that you and your client are working *together*. The latter communication is important because many clients will experience a disclosure as a rift, a break in the relationship, perhaps even a betrayal of faith. By emphasizing at the beginning of your work that any such disclosure will be done in the interests of your work and that it will be done *with* the client, you are "vaccinating" your treatment, as it were, against such an injury. Other clients will necessitate other emphases. If, for example, you are working with a parent who is considering a divorce and with whose family DSS has become involved, you will want to explain that should custody of the children become an issue, some of what you talk about may be disclosed for a court proceeding. It's important to address the issue at the beginning of your work, in a way that speaks to your client.

A note to psychologists and social workers: The language of your confidentiality laws is explicit about discussing the limitations to confidentiality at the "initiation of the professional relationship." In addition, the

Massachusetts regulation that governs confidential communications for psychologists, 251 CMR 1.11 (found in appendix A), emphasizes the importance of discussing all exceptions to confidentiality at this time. The difficulty is that, were a psychologist or social worker overly concrete, the first session would consist of nothing *other* than a discussion of the exceptions to confidentiality. Moreover, if you actually used the entire first session in this manner, it would be highly doubtful that you would have a second session with any but the most masochistic of clients. Our recommendation is to consider using an informed consent letter, which you can give to your client at the first session. Such a letter, while by no means problem-free, has a number of advantages (see part II, question 108 and, for a sample letter, appendix B). If you decide not to use a letter, it is essential that you document the discussion in which you obtain informed consent from your client.

The fifth noteworthy element concerns a provision in the psychologist statute. This provision reads, "the psychologist shall only disclose that information which is essential in order to protect the rights and safety of others." This is yet another example of a clause that should be understood to apply to all mental health professionals. Like the clause that requires a discussion of the limits of confidentiality, the idea behind this clause is sufficiently important that we make it into a principle, "The Parsimony Principle." The Parsimony Principle says that a mental health professional only discloses that information necessary to get the job done, and no more. If, for example, you receive a call from an emergency room physician who needs to have certain information about a suicidal client, you provide information that will help the physician assess and formulate a plan to protect your client's safety. No more. If you are making a referral for an MRI, you may choose to share that your client suffers from an anxiety disorder, since her anxiety may make it difficult for her to tolerate lying in a long, dark tube. There is no reason to share that she also suffers from an eating disorder. To put the Parsimony Principle another way: Determine what information is necessary and sufficient to address the need for disclosure, and disclose only that information. The Law of No Surprises and the Parsimony Principle are guides for all mental health professionals when they must disclose confidential information.

One last point. Every mental health professional must look to her profession's code of ethics before disclosing confidential information. Each major mental health discipline has its own code of ethics, and every ethics code speaks to the issue of confidentiality and confidential communications. If, in disclosing confidential information, a mental health professional violates that code, she runs several risks: that of being disciplined by her professional association; that of being considered negligent for deviating from her profession's standard of care; that of violating a state regulation, if the state regulations incorporate a code of ethics, as the Code of Massachusetts Regulations incorporates the American Psychological Association's Code of Ethics (APA, 1992). *Read and become familiar with your profession's code of ethics.*

We now turn to a discussion of specific circumstances in which disclosures of confidential information are permitted or required: These are the exceptions to confidentiality. Note that, because testimonial privilege is a subset of confidentiality, we include in our discussion the exceptions to testimonial privilege as well. The exceptions are those circumstances in which society has decided that the importance of some interest or value outweighs the value of confidentiality.

CONFIDENTIALITY: DISCLOSURES OF INFORMATION

I. Law of No Surprises
   A. Inform client at outset that there are limits to confidentiality.
      1. Give general contours of limits to confidentiality at initial session.
      2. Tailor what you say to meet needs and circumstances of specific client.
      3. Emphasize that client will be notified of any disclosures.
      4. Psychologists and social workers have higher duty to discuss limits of confidentiality at initial meeting.
      5. Document your discussion.
   B. Whenever possible, make client part of disclosure process, up to and including having the client make the actual disclosure when appropriate.
   C. Consider giving client informed consent letter at first session.

II. Parsimony Principle
   A. Determine what information is necessary and sufficient to meet purpose of disclosure.
   B. Disclose only that information.

III. Professional codes of ethics

EXCEPTIONS TO CONFIDENTIALITY

In the past few years many people have argued that confidentiality is more the exception than the rule. Despite appearances, confidentiality is maintained in the majority of treatments conducted by mental health professionals. Essential to your work, however, is a clear understanding of when you are *not* bound by confidentiality and when you are bound to *break* confidentiality.

Keep in mind that every exception to confidentiality represents a balance of some value against the value of keeping clinical material confidential. Put another way, every time there is an occasion to disclose confidential information to third parties, *there is another interest at stake that trumps confidentiality.* If you can hold onto this point as you read through the exceptions to confidentiality, you are well on your way to understanding this area of law. The permissive and mandatory exceptions to confidentiality include:

1. client consent
2. emergencies
3. exceptions in the confidentiality statutes and regulations
4. exceptions in the testimonial privilege statutes
5. exceptions for psychiatric inpatients
6. sex offender registry exception for DMH clients
7. mandatory reporting statutes

An outline of the essential elements of the exceptions to confidentiality is found on pages 48–49)

CLIENT CONSENT
The value behind confidentiality is individual autonomy. Autonomy dictates that an individual is free to decide for herself with whom she will communicate and what the content of her communications will be. The first exception to the rule of confidentiality is entirely consistent with individual autonomy: An adult client who is competent may *consent* to allow the mental health professional to share communications with specified third parties. In the case of client consent, the disclosure of information furthers the client's wishes, and so reinforces the value of individual autonomy.

Each of the statutes names client consent as an exception to confidentiality, and this underscores an important, yet often overlooked, point: Confidentiality belongs to *the client.* Consistent with the value of autonomy, in the vast majority of cases it is for your client—not you—to decide with whom to share otherwise confidential information. When your client is a couple or a family, you should get the consent of each adult participant before disclosing any information, a requirement stated in the social worker (c.112, §135A) and allied mental health and human services confidentiality (c.112, §172) statutes, but a requirement that should be understood to apply to all mental health professionals.

The statutes state that the consent must be "written." It is always preferable to obtain written consent, insofar as a written consent makes clear the nature and extent of the consent and will serve as a record if any unclarity or disagreement about the consent arises. When obtaining written consent, try to specify as best you can the nature and extent of the information that may be disclosed, the individual or agency to whom the disclosure may be made, the date on which the disclosure becomes valid, and the date on which the disclosure ceases to be valid.

In practice, many clinicians, especially when they have a good working relationship with a client, rely on an oral consent, and perhaps would even consider it patronizing or demeaning to ask a client to sign a release. The vast majority of these clinicians will never encounter any clinical or legal difficulties from their practice. Important to remember, though, is that should any misunderstanding arise, the dispute will degenerate into the clinician's word against that of the client, a position in which no clinician would want to find herself. At the very least, the clinician will want to document the patient's oral consent.

EMERGENCIES

The second exception to confidentiality, that of an emergency, is likewise consistent with the value of autonomy. Whereas client consent is the direct expression of a client's wishes, the disclosure of confidential information in an emergency is *presumed* to be the expression of a client's wishes. The presumption is that most people would give the emergency precedence over confidentiality. This presumption is honored for the duration of the emergency—even if the client expressly states a wish that confidentiality *not* be broken. The idea behind this exception is that an emergency is no time to sort these things out, to decide whether a client's judgment is intact or whether his words are a true expression of his desires—all that can wait until after the emergency is resolved. During the course of the emergency, confidentiality will yield to safety; that is the way most people would want it.

The psychologist and social worker statutes provide guidance in defining "emergency." First, they say that confidentiality may be broken when information is needed to protect "the rights and safety" of individuals. "Safety" is the operative word here, and we should consider an emergency to be a circumstance that implicates safety. Next, theses two statutes incorporate the Massachusetts *Tarasoff* statute into their language; confidentiality is broken when there is threat of death or serious bodily injury. Finally, confidentiality is broken when "the patient presents a clear and present danger to himself." The language of these statutes gives the term "emergency" contours—an emergency is a circumstance in which information is necessary to protect safety, to prevent serious bodily injury, or to avert a clear and present danger. Certainly many of these words, "safety," "danger," even "injury," are susceptible to multiple interpretations. In practice, however, you can go by the rule that an emergency is a circumstance in which a reasonable person would judge that an individual's physical safety is at risk. You may disclose confidential information for the purpose of attenuating that risk; let the Parsimony Principle be your guide as you do so.

Four other points about the emergency exception to confidentiality merit discussion. Note first that, in practice, "safety" will cover more situations than merely those in which an individual intentionally harms himself or someone else. Safety is at issue whenever an individual's physical health or integrity is threatened, regardless of the source of the threat. For example, if you receive a call from an emergency room physician because your client is having a serious physical problem, you may reveal what medications your client is taking, because such information is necessary for the treatment.

Second, the psychologist and social work statutes state explicitly that when a client presents a danger to himself, the psychologist or social worker may "contact members of the [client's] family or other individuals" if doing so is necessary to protect the client's safety. The spirit behind this language is that safety trumps. When your client's safety is at issue, and to protect that safety it is necessary to contact friends or family, do so.

Third, beware of strangers claiming "emergency." Many a clinician has been duped into disclosing confidential information by a caller stating that an emergency necessitates releasing client information. Before discussing any client on an emergency basis, ask *who* needs to know, and *what emergency* necessitates disclosure. If a true emergency exists, this information can be passed on in a matter of a few seconds. If you have doubts, attempt to confirm the emergency before discussing your client.*

Finally, when faced with a possible emergency, *pay attention to the process by which you decide what to do.* Your protection from a breach-of-confidentiality claim will be your documentation of the process by which you come to a decision about whether to break or to maintain your client's confidentiality. As your decision-making process unfolds, you should consider the facts as they are known to you; the reliability of your sources; the imminence of harm; alternatives to breaking confidentiality; consultations which, in an ambiguous situation, agree with the degree of the emergency and the necessity of breaking confidentiality. Your documentation should indicate that you have made a reasoned decision about what to do—what will *not* help is a note in the record that reads, "Emergency, disclosed confidential patient information." Although there may be very good reasons for doing so, your protection from liability—the documentation of how you came to your decision—is nowhere to be found in such a note.

EXCEPTIONS IN THE CONFIDENTIALITY STATUTES
AND REGULATIONS

Exceptions to client confidentiality also arise from the confidentiality statutes and regulations. Note that many exceptions found in confidentiality statutes and regulations are really nothing other than variations on themes we have already discussed, most notably safety, emergency, and client consent. As you read on, the material may seem somewhat redundant—that's because it is. Keep reading anyway.

The first exception is safety, and can be considered to fall under the emergency exception, discussed above, and the *Tarasoff* statute, discussed in chapter 1. This exception, while mentioned explicitly only in the psychologist and social work statutes, applies to all mental health professionals. You may release information to prevent harm to your client, or to prevent your client from inflicting harm on some other individual, if the criteria spelled out in the statutes are met. If the disclosure is to assist in protecting the safety of your patient, you may contact the patient's family or other individuals. Again, your best protection from liability is your *documentation of the process* by which you have decided whether to break or to maintain confidentiality.

---

* We owe a debt to Jay Patel, M.D., for emphasizing this important point to us.

The second exception arises when a client does not pay for services. At the outset, the psychologist or social worker may divulge "the nature of the services provided, the dates of the services, the amount due for services and other relevant financial information." This rule follows the Parsimony Principle: Disclose only that information necessary to accomplish your purpose. In this case, your purpose is to get paid. If your client raises questions concerning the competence or quality of the treatment, you may then "disclose whatever information is necessary to rebut such assertions." This clause expands the amount of information you may disclose, but note that it, too, will follow the Parsimony Principle. The idea behind this exception is straightforward: A client should not be allowed to use confidentiality to shield himself from fulfilling his contractual obligations, in this case paying an agreed upon fee.*

A third exception found in the confidentiality statutes involves insurance benefits. At the end of the psychologist and social worker statutes, you will find a clause stating that records may be inspected for the purpose of determining eligibility or entitlement to benefits, "so long as the policy or certificate under which the claim is made provides that such access to such records is permitted." Note that, in virtue of this clause, this exception is really a matter of client consent. Before releasing any information to an insurance company, however, you *must have a release signed by the patient.* (See part II, question 119 for a further discussion of what may be released to an insurance company.)

A fourth exception pertains only to allied mental health and human services professionals and social workers. Allied mental health and human services professionals (licensed marriage and family therapists, licensed rehabilitation counselors, licensed educational psychologists, licensed mental health counselors) and social workers are not bound by confidentiality when the communication "reveals the contemplation or commission of a crime or a harmful act." The statute does not obligate these mental health professionals to disclose the communication. It says merely that they are not bound to keep such communications confidential. Note that the "or" joining "harmful act" and "crime" distinguishes crime from harmful act, thus making clear that the crime does not need to entail harm in order to fall within this exception. (See part II, question 87 for a further discussion of this exception.)

Finally, social workers may disclose information in the course of con-

---

* We recommend a *very* judicious use of this exception (see part II, question 126).

ducting investigations for the Department of Social Services, the Disabled Persons Protection Commission, and elderly protective agencies. These exceptions are based on the special role of social workers in protecting groups of individuals who are often not able to protect themselves.

EXCEPTIONS IN THE TESTIMONIAL PRIVILEGE STATUTES

The next exceptions to confidentiality arise from the testimonial privilege statutes. While confidentiality statutes for certain disciplines, such as allied mental health professionals, speak to the issue of testimonial privilege, only two disciplines have statutes for privilege separate from their confidentiality statutes: *psychotherapists*, a term that includes psychiatrists, licensed psychologists, and licensed psychiatric nurses (c.233, §20B), and *social workers* (c.112, §135B). The six exceptions found in these statutes would perhaps more appropriately be called "potential exceptions." The reason for this qualification is that no exception to testimonial privilege is automatic. When the possibility of an exception is raised, a judge will review the materials in his office (called an "in camera" inspection) to see if the materials are relevant to the matter at hand. If the judge decides that the materials are relevant, and that one of the exceptions to privilege applies, the judge will issue an order that the materials be introduced into the legal proceeding. If the judge decides that the materials are not relevant, or that no exception to privilege applies, the materials will be excluded from the proceeding.

Before we begin our discussion of the exceptions to privilege, remember that a client may always consent to have communications revealed in a legal proceeding. In this case, the client is said to "waive privilege." If the treatment involves a couple or a family, the psychotherapist statute makes clear that *each* adult in the treatment must waive privilege before communications may be revealed. Family and couples therapists need to exercise caution when, in the midst of a divorce or separation, one parent requests treatment records; no records should be released until *both* parents waive privilege.*

---

* Two possible exceptions to this rule arise: first, when the records can be redacted, so that *no* information other than that pertaining to the child and the parent signing the release is available to the reader; and second, when separate records are kept for each patient. In both of these cases, an argument can be made that each participant in the therapy need not waive privilege. Given the explicit language of the statute, however, it would be wise to consult with an attorney before actually disclosing information without each participant's waiver.

The first exception to privilege arises when a client is "in need of treatment" or when "there is a threat of imminently dangerous activity." In these instances the mental health professional may break confidentiality "for the purpose of placing or retaining the client" in a hospital. Note how closely this language resembles the language found in both the psychologist and social work confidentiality statutes, as well as the language found in the *Tarasoff* statute. The important point is that if your client needs treatment or is dangerous, you may disclose information to get your client into a hospital by way of a "pink paper" (see part II, question 31).

The second exception arises when a court has ordered a psychiatric examination. This exception is premised *upon the mental health professional having informed the client that his communications are not confidential.* If, for example, a mental health professional is asked by a court to examine a criminal defendant, for the purpose of determining whether the defendant was sane at the time of a crime, the mental health professional must tell the client that their conversation will not be kept in confidence. If the mental health professional fails in this regard, the client's testimony cannot be admitted into evidence. Note how this exception is really a variation on client consent. If the mental health professional does not explain the purpose of the examination, namely, that it is to be used in court, the client will be deemed *not* to have consented to the disclosure, and the examination cannot be submitted in the legal proceeding. Informing the client that discussions will be not be kept confidential is referred to as giving a "Lamb warning," so named for the Supreme Judicial Court case *Commonwealth v. Lamb,* 368 Mass. 491 (1975).

The third and fourth exceptions arise when a client's mental or emotional state is introduced in court. The third exception arises when a client is alive; a common scenario would be when a client claims that he has suffered severe emotional distress after an accident. A fourth exception arises following a client's death. Say, for example, an individual claims that her father was not competent when he wrote his will, or an insurance company believes that an accident was actually a suicide. In each of these cases, a judge may decide that, for the sake of justice, a mental health professional must reveal confidential communications.

The fifth exception arises in the course of custody or adoption proceedings. A judge may determine that confidential information must be reviewed by the court as it determines what is best for the child. As with the case of psychiatric examinations ordered by the court, however, the client must be told that his communications would not be confidential; otherwise they are not admissible, and privilege holds. Again we see the importance of client consent.

The sixth exception to testimonial privilege arises when a client sues, or otherwise brings a legal action against a mental health professional. If confidential information is necessary, or even relevant, to the mental health professional's defense, it may be introduced at a legal proceeding. The law will thus not permit a client to use testimonial privilege as a way of rendering the mental health professional defenseless against the client's accusation.

EXCEPTIONS FOR PSYCHIATRIC INPATIENTS

A special set of exceptions to confidentiality applies to psychiatric inpatients. Section 36 of chapter 123 states that inpatient records may be released to a third party when "in the best interest" of the patient. The regulation written pursuant to chapter 123, section 36, 104 CMR 27.18(6), gives several examples of the "best interest" rule: when the records are necessary to pursue or defend against a legal claim, to enforce a civil right, or to obtain third party payments. In addition, 104 CMR 27.18(6) states that the release of records is in the patient's best interest in an emergency, when the patient is being transferred from one facility to another, or when the Department of Mental Health is conducting an investigation into an incident involving harm to the patient.

SEX OFFENDER REGISTRY EXCEPTION FOR DMH CLIENTS

The Sex Offenders Registry Law, M.G.L. chapter 6, sections 178C–178O, requires that the Department of Mental Health release records for certain DMH clients who have been involved with the legal system because of sexual offenses. Note that *when material is released pursuant to the Sex Offenders Registry Law, the DMH, rather than a clinician, will make the actual disclosure.* It is important for the clinician to be aware of which clients are affected by this law, insofar as the treatment record may be subject to review by the Sex Offender Registry Board when it classifies the client's level of risk for offending again.

The final set of exceptions to client confidentiality arises from the mandatory reporting statutes. We now turn to the Commonwealth's four mandatory reporting statutes.

MANDATORY REPORTING STATUTES

To the extent the law serves as a balance for competing interests, mandatory reporting statutes provide an excellent illustration of our jurisprudence at work. Mandatory reporting statutes require that information pertaining to certain groups of individuals *not* be kept confidential. These are groups that society has deemed particularly vulnerable—children, the elderly, disabled individuals, and individuals in need of inpatient or residential care. Because these groups are less able to protect themselves than other groups in society, we place a higher value on ensuring their health and well-being than we do on keeping information revealed in a clinical setting confidential. As a consequence, information about harm or abuse to individuals in these groups is made available to agencies charged with their protection. Mandatory reporting statutes make clear the societal balance of values: For individuals belonging to especially vulnerable groups, well-being and safety trump confidentiality.

A brief note before we begin. We have not included M.G.L. chapter 123, section 36B, the *Tarasoff* statute (see chapter 2), in our discussion. M.G.L. chapter 123, section 36B is different from the four mandatory reporting statutes because it makes available to a clinician several options (the four "reasonable precautions"); indeed, attempting to persuade the client to enter a hospital voluntarily is an acceptable response to the conditions that give rise to a duty under the statute. Nevertheless, a clinician will want to be clear that a duty does arise under the *Tarasoff* statute, a duty that may require a disclosure of information to protect safety. If, for example, the client must be "pink papered" into a hospital, the treating clinician will want to make the threat known to the inpatient treatment team so that the team will know what to treat. The important point is to identify what disclosure is necessary to protect an identified victim of harm. The statute creates a duty for the clinician to disclose *that* information.

The four mandatory reporting statutes are remarkably similar in both structure and content. We will comment upon nine elements of these statutes.

The central elements of the Commonwealth's mandatory reporting laws are found in appendix A. An outline of the essential elements of the mandatory reporting laws is found on pages 47–48.

The first of the nine elements is perhaps the most obvious, and for that reason all the more likely to be overlooked: Individuals are *required* to report when certain criteria are met. That is why these statutes are called "mandatory," rather than "discretionary," reporting statutes. Unlike the *Tarasoff* statute, these statutes do not provide the mental health professional with a list of options, "reasonable precautions," from which a mental health professional may fashion an appropriate response. Rather, they are quite specific about both the mandatory nature of the reporting, and the nature, circumstances, and timing of the report that must be made.

The second of the nine elements is the list of mental health professionals upon whom the statutes impose a duty to report. This list, found at the beginning of each of the statutes, covers most anyone who would come into contact with the individuals at issue. Of special note is the length of the list in the child-reporting statute; this list serves as an impressive statement as to how seriously the legislature takes this matter—virtually anyone who, in a professional capacity, comes into contact with children is a mandated reporter. Note also that, in addition to mandating that certain individuals report, the statutes also *permit* any individual to report. The permissive element is expansive, insofar as there are no restrictions on who may file. Thus, the statutes have both mandatory and permissive elements. Certain individuals *must* report, any other individual *may* report.

The third element involves the definition of the four groups of individuals. *A child* is defined as anyone under 18 years of age, while an *elderly person* is any individual 60 years of age or older. The definition of *disabled person* has three elements: The person is between the ages of 18 and 59, the person has some mental or physical disability, and, as a result of the mental or physical disability, the person "is wholly or partially dependent upon others to meet his daily living needs." Note how the first two groups are defined solely by age, while the third is defined by a dependency that stems from a disability. The final reporting statute provides no definition, other than that an individual is a *patient or resident* at a facility. This group, therefore, resembles the group of disabled persons, insofar as it is the status of needing assistance that merits the need for mandatory reporting.

The fourth element involves the definition of the conditions that must be reported. For children these conditions are "physical or emotional injury . . . which causes harm or substantial risk of harm to the child's health or welfare including sexual abuse, or . . . neglect, including malnutrition, or . . . [physical] dependen[ce] upon an addictive drug at birth."

For children, that is, individuals under 18 years of age, injuries that cause harm or substantial *risk* of harm, sexual abuse, or addiction at birth are the conditions to be reported. For the elderly, the definition of abuse is "an act . . . which results in serious physical or emotional injury . . . or financial exploitation." The definition of abuse is both narrower than that for children, insofar as the injury must be "serious," and more expansive, insofar as abuse may also consist of "financial exploitation." See how the legislature, in recognizing that the elderly are especially vulnerable to financial exploitation, is tailoring the statute to the needs of the particular population. The definition of "abuse" for disabled persons involves "serious physical or emotional injury" as well as "unconsented to sexual activity." This more limited scope of reportable conditions reflects the legislature's assessment that because disabled persons are generally competent and so less in need of protection, the law should be less willing to override their confidentiality. At the same time, including "unconsented to sexual activity" as a reportable condition recognizes the special vulnerability of these individuals. The statute for patients or residents at a facility states that abuse, mistreatment, or neglect constitute reportable conditions. The Massachusetts legislature once again recognizes the unique characteristics of this population by defining mistreatment as the "use of medications, isolation, or use of physical or chemical restraints which harms or is likely to harm the patient or resident."

The fifth element identifies the standard by which reports must be made. Each of the statutes uses exactly the same wording here: "reasonable cause to believe." The statutes do not require that a reporter know definitively, or confirm, that the reportable condition—be it abuse, neglect, maltreatment, unconsented to sexual activity, or financial exploitation—is occurring. Rather, the statutes only require that the reporter have *reasonable cause to believe* that the necessary conditions are present. This represents a conscious decision of the legislature. Once a reporter has reasonable cause to believe, the reporter will turn the matter over to a state agency that will initiate an investigation. This wording encourages reporters to act without waiting for definitive evidence, thus *increasing* the likelihood that a report will be made. Consistent with this wording, the Attorney General (in a written opinion dated May 27, 1975) has determined that individuals mandated to report should have a low threshold for reporting.

The sixth element involves the timing of the report. Each of the four statutes require two sorts of report: an oral report and a written report.

The oral report must be made "immediately," while the written report must be made within 48 hours. Reports about children go to the Department of Social Services (DSS; 1-800-792-5200); reports about disabled persons are made to the Disabled Persons Protection Commission (DPPC; 1-800-426-9009); reports about the elderly go to the Department of Elderly Affairs (1-800-922–2275); reports about patients or residents in a facility go to the Department of Public Health (1-800-462-5540). Reports about children can be made in one of two ways. If the reporter is an employee of an institution such as a day care center, school, or hospital, the reporter may either report the suspected abuse directly to the Department of Social Services or, in the alternative, to the head of the institution, who then has the responsibility for reporting to the Department of Social Services. The statutes explain in detail what information must go into the written report so that the relevant state agency can move forward with its investigation.

The seventh element is the penalties for not reporting when one is mandated to do so, and release from liability when a report is actually made. Each statute states that a mandated reporter with reasonable cause to believe who does not report may be fined up to one thousand dollars. Each statute likewise releases from liability any individual who makes a report in good faith. The clear message is that penalties will attach if a reporter has reasonable cause to suspect abuse and does nothing, whereas such an individual who goes forward in accordance with the law and contacts the appropriate agency will not incur a penalty. In addition, each statute states that no reprisals, economic or otherwise, may be made against an individual who appropriately makes a report.

The eighth element involves the waiver of confidentiality. Each of the statutes states that any individual who makes a report is not bound by confidentiality or privilege. This provision makes explicit the balance of values behind this set of laws: Confidentiality will yield when the health, well-being, and safety of individuals whom we deem especially vulnerable and in need of protection are at issue.

The ninth, and final, element concerns a special provision in the disabled person statute. The statute states that "a mandated reporter need not report an otherwise reportable condition if the disabled person invokes a privilege." This provision sets the disabled persons reporting statute apart from the other mandatory reporting statutes by vesting in the disabled person the right to invoke privilege. If the client invokes privi-

MANDATORY REPORTING STATUTES

I. Mandate reporting for certain groups:
   A. Children (individuals under the age of 18) (M.G.L. c.119, §51A)
   B. Elderly (individuals 60 or over) (M.G.L. c.19A, §§14 and 15)
   C. Disabled persons (persons between the ages of 18 and 59 who are disabled and, as a result of the disability, are dependent upon others) (M.G.L. c.19C, §§1, 10, and 11)
   D. Patients or residents at a health care facility (M.G.L. c.111, §§72F and 72G)

II. Conditions for reporting:
   A. Children
      1. Physical or emotional injury which causes harm or substantial risk of harm
      2. Sexual abuse
      3. Neglect
      4. Physical dependence upon addictive drug at birth
   B. Elderly
      1. Serious physical or emotional injury
      2. Financial exploitation
   C. Disabled persons
      1. Serious physical or emotional injury resulting from abuse
      2. Unconsented to sexual activity
   D. Patients or residents
      1. Abuse and neglect
      2. Mistreatment, the "use of medications, isolation, or use of physical or chemical restraints which harms or is likely to harm the patient or resident"

III. Standard for reporting: *Reasonable cause to believe* condition for reporting is present

IV. When reports must be made:
   A. Oral reports (immediately)
   B. Written reports (within 48 hours)

V. To whom reports must be made when report involves:
   A. Children (Department of Social Services/Head of the Institution, who makes report to the Department of Social Services) (1-800-792-5200)
   B. Elderly (Department of Elderly Affairs) (1-800-922-2275)
   C. Disabled persons (Disabled Person Protection Commission) (1-800-426-9009)
   D. Patients or residents (Department of Public Health) (1-800-462-5540)

continued

MANDATORY REPORTING STATUTES, *continued*

VI.   Fine for not reporting: One thousand dollars

VII.   Release from liability: No civil or criminal sanctions attach when report is made in good faith

VIII.   Reporters not bound by:
- A.   Confidentiality or testimonial privilege
- B.   When reporting involves disabled person, and disabled person invokes privilege, mental health professional no longer a mandatory reporter.

IX.   Consider whether duty arises from c.123, §36B (*Tarasoff* statute): When there is an identified victim of client's harm.

---

lege, the mental health professional is no longer a mandatory reporter. The assumption is that disabled persons are competent—dependency, the defining element in the definition of a disabled person, does not mean that an individual is not competent to make decisions about how best to protect his or her own interests. While the language of the statute is somewhat ambiguous about what happens when a disabled person invokes privilege, our recommendation is the following: If a treater has "reasonable cause to suspect" that a disabled client has suffered abuse, discuss the matter with the client. Ask the client permission to inform the DPPC. If the client grants permission, document your discussion and make a report. If a client invokes privilege, document that he has done so, then

---

EXCEPTIONS TO CONFIDENTIALITY

(All disclosures follow the Law of No Surprises, the Parsimony Principle, and professional codes of ethics)

I.   Client consent
- A.   Should be in writing
- B.   Obtain from each adult participant in treatment

II. Emergency
- A.   At issue: serious bodily injury, clear and present danger
- B.   May contact members of patient's family or other individuals *if necessary*
- C.   Documentation of decision-making process critical

continued

III. Exceptions to confidentiality created by statute and regulation:
A. Safety and *Tarasoff* issues
B. Client does not pay for services
   1. May initially disclose relevant financial information
   2. May disclose "whatever information necessary to rebut such assertions" if client challenges competence or quality of treatment
C. Insurance policy *with the patient's signed release*
D. "Contemplation or commission or a crime or harmful act" (*for allied health and human services professionals and social workers only*)
E. Investigations into abuse of children, the elderly, and disabled persons (*social workers only, although mental health professionals may be required to report abuse to the appropriate investigative agency*)

IV. Six exceptions to testimonial privilege created by statute:
A. Patient in need of treatment, or there is threat of imminently dangerous activity
B. Statements made in course of psychiatric examination ordered by court, *provided patient has been informed that the communications would not be kept confidential*
C. Patient introduces mental or emotional condition into legal proceeding
D. Patient's mental or emotional condition introduced into legal proceeding following patient's death
E. Custody or adoption proceedings, *provided patient has been informed that the communications would not be kept confidential*
F. Patient brings legal action against mental health professional

V. Exceptions for psychiatric inpatients:
A. Records may be released when in patient's "best interest"
B. CMR provides examples of "best interest"

VI. Sex Offender Registry exception for Department of Mental Health clients:
A. DMH, rather than the clinician, actually releases the records
B. Treatment records may be subject to review by Sex Offender Registry Board

VII. Mandatory reporting statutes
A. Children
B. Elderly
C. Disabled persons
D. Patients or residents
E. Possible mandatory reporting: when client has identified victim of harm

keep the matter within the therapy relationship and do not report to the DPPC. By following this advice, you both fulfill the requirements of the statute and respect your patient's autonomy, competence, and right to confidentiality.

Part I, our introduction to the law, closes here. Part II, 150 Questions on Massachusetts Mental Health Law, is really nothing more than the application of the concepts put forth in the first part of the book. As you read part II, keep in mind that behind every statute or regulation lies an important value; behind every exception to a statute or regulation lies another important value.

When faced with a problem that has no clear solution, think through what values are at stake. Remember as you do so that any statute or regulation can be analyzed in the same way as we've done in chapters 2 and 3. If you can break a law down into its smaller parts, the law's mystique will soon evaporate. So will lingering anxieties about your legal rights and responsibilities.

Part II

150 Questions on Massachusetts Mental Health law

Part II consists of 150 questions mental health professionals often ask about the law. For the most part, the questions are self-explanatory, so only a brief word of introduction is in order.

First, our questions represent a fraction of what could be asked—the list is virtually endless. What we have done is to divide the questions into ten chapters—or topics—that cover the essential areas of mental health law, and then to present those questions that, in our experience, most concern clinicians. Familiarity with the answers will provide an excellent overview of what clinicians need to know in Massachusetts. If, after reading part II, you don't have a particular answer you are looking for, you will at the very least have a way to think about the question, which is often nearly as good as having the answer itself.

Second, the questions refer to a number of statutes, regulations, and court cases. We thought, therefore, it would be helpful to review how Massachusetts laws are cited:

- Statutes: M.G.L. c.123, §36B refers to Massachusetts General Laws, chapter 123, section 36B.

- Cases of the Massachusetts Supreme Judicial Court (SJC): *Rogers v. Commissioner of the Department of Mental Health,* 390 Mass. 489 (1983) refers to SJC *Rogers* opinion, written in 1983, found in the *Massachusetts Reports,* on page 489 of volume 390.
- Cases of the Massachusetts Appeals Court: *Bak v. Bak,* 24 Mass. App. Ct. 608 (1987) refers to the *Bak* opinion of the Appeals Court, found in the *Massachusetts Appeals Court Reports,* on page 608 of volume 24.
- Code of Massachusetts Regulations: 104 CMR 27.05 refers to the Code of Massachusetts Regulations, chapter 104, section 27.05.

Finally, don't read all the questions at once. It's too much. Part II covers a lot of territory, much more than can be absorbed in one sitting. At most, read a single topic heading at a time. Responses are designed for easy access, and are well-suited as references—but they can be dense. Take your time, enjoy what you read, and let us know what you think. Part II of this book will serve its purpose well if you find these questions, and our responses, helpful in your clinical practice.

4

THE LEGAL SYSTEM AND LEGAL PROCESS

Mental health professionals find no topic more shrouded in mystery than the legal system and legal process: the law's way of doing things. Remember, though, that lawyers find what mental health professionals do equally mystifying—and intriguing. The questions below, which discuss particular aspects of how the legal system works, are written to illuminate the method behind the law's seeming madness. As you read, try to keep in mind both the legal rule and whatever value the rule, or its exception, is designed to promote.

QUESTIONS DISCUSSED IN THIS CHAPTER

1. What is the difference between civil law and criminal law?
2. What is a tort?
3. What does it mean to say that our system of law is "adversarial"?
4. What is a standard of proof?
5. What does it mean to say that a court has "jurisdiction"?
6. Why do lawyers seem so different than mental health professionals?
7. What is a deposition?

8. Why is a deposition important?
9. What are interrogatories?
10. What is the difference between an expert witness and a fact witness?
11. How is it decided who will be an expert witness?
12. If I receive a subpoena and must testify at a deposition about a therapy case, am I an expert witness or a fact witness?
13. What should I know if I am called to testify as a fact witness?
14. Does whether I am an expert witness or a fact witness make any difference in how much I am paid?
15. What is a statute of limitations?
16. What is the statute of limitations for malpractice lawsuits in Massachusetts?
17. Do licensing boards have statutes of limitations?
18. What is the discovery rule?
19. How do the statute of limitations and the discovery rule apply to cases involving minors?
20. What is the Medical Malpractice Tribunal?
21. What is the Americans with Disabilities Act?

DISCUSSION

1. What is the difference between civil law and criminal law?

Criminal law is based on the notion of *moral blameworthiness*. In a criminal court a person may be found "guilty," given a fine, and sentenced to jail or prison because he has violated the criminal law and so must be morally sanctioned. Murder and manslaughter are two examples of crimes for which society punishes wrongdoers.

Civil law is much further removed from the notion of moral blameworthiness. The purpose of a lawsuit in a civil court is to apportion responsibility in order to make an injured party whole. Thus, a suit in malpractice serves the purpose of determining whether a treater is responsible—in civil court parlance, "liable"—for the injury suffered by a patient. If the treater is found liable, the civil court will then determine what will be required to remedy that injury, that is, what will be required to make the patient whole. The remedy is referred to as the "award."

2. What is a tort?

In the words of Black's Law Dictionary, a tort is a "private or civil wrong or injury . . . for which a court will provide a remedy in the form of an action for damages." To explain, a tort is a *civil* (as opposed to *criminal*) wrong—a private individual has been injured and goes to court in order to seek compensation. At times the parties to an action in tort will agree to *settle* the matter, in which case they agree upon some amount of damages without waiting for a court to decide. Malpractice is a form of tort. (The elements of a malpractice claim are discussed in chapter 2).

3. What does it mean to say that our system of law is "adversarial"?

Cases in law, whether civil or criminal, pit one party against another. The parties to a lawsuit are thus *adversaries*. Our adversarial system of law is built on the assumption that having two parties on opposite sides of an issue is the way most likely to yield what is true, right, and fair. In criminal cases, one party is the government. The idea is that an individual has harmed society as a whole by his crime, and the government has the responsibility of ensuring that the individual is held accountable for what he has done. Note how, by taking on this responsibility, the government also precludes private individuals from exacting retribution—vengeance belongeth to the state. Thus, the title of a criminal case is always along the lines of *State of Texas v. Saks*, showing that the State of Texas is the aggrieved party bringing suit. Saks is the criminal defendant, who may go to jail if she is found guilty. (The State of Texas is referred to as "the prosecution" or simply as "the State.") In civil law, private individuals who have been harmed may bring the action, and are referred to as "plaintiffs." The second name in the title of both civil and criminal lawsuits, the name on the other side of the *v.* (for "versus") is the "defendant." What's important to remember is that lawsuits consist of *adversaries*, two parties with competing interests, only one of whom will prevail.

4. What is a standard of proof?

Think of a standard of proof as being like a hurdle. If anyone told you that on your way to work tomorrow you'd have to jump over a hurdle, you might well ask, "How high of a hurdle?" Exactly the same question is asked in law. The "height" of the hurdle in a legal proceeding depends on the importance of the matter at hand. Criminal trials, at which the defendant's personal liberty is at stake, require the highest standard of proof in our adversarial system, proof *beyond a reasonable doubt*. The prosecution, that is, the attorney working for the government, must show beyond a reasonable doubt that the individual committed the crime. The reason for this high hurdle is that in our society, we will deprive an individual of his liberty only when we are certain of his guilt. The height of the hurdle thus reflects our values. While proof beyond a reasonable doubt is considered proof in the 99% range, proof *by clear and convincing evidence* is considered to be proof in the 75% range. The lowest standard of proof, *a preponderance of the evidence,* is 51%, referred to simply as *more likely than not.* When a malpractice case goes to court, the plaintiff—the person bringing the lawsuit—must prove his case by a preponderance of the evidence. Standards of proof are determined by statute. Any legal proceeding will involve a standard of proof, and a mental health professional who becomes involved will want to know, "What's the burden of proof to be met?" or, in other words, "How high of a hurdle must the plaintiff jump to win his case?"

5. What does it mean to say that a court has "jurisdiction"?
Jurisdiction is the legal way of saying "who gets to decide." The person with the T.V. clicker has jurisdiction over which programs are watched; the person in the driver's seat has jurisdiction over what radio station is played in the car; the birthday boy or girl has jurisdiction over what kind of cake gets served. Jurisdiction indicates in whose domain a particular matter rests. Generally, a statute will indicate which court has jurisdiction over a given matter. Massachusetts statutes, for example, provide that the probate court has jurisdiction over guardianships, the superior court has jurisdiction over malpractice cases, and the district court has jurisdiction over petitions for involuntary civil commitment. The point is, before beginning a legal proceeding a party must determine which court has jurisdiction; that is, which court gets to decide. Only then can the parties move forward toward settling their disagreement.

6. Why do lawyers seem so different than mental health professionals?
Lawyers, by training, are professional skeptics who take nothing at face value and will insist that a mental health professional support a position by concrete evidence. To complicate matters, lawyers see themselves as representing what the patient wants, which, to a lawyer, translates into what the patient *says* he wants at a given point in time.

The skepticism displayed by lawyers is part of their professional training and serves them well in legal proceedings, where evidence must be supported by standards of proof. Recall that the *lowest* standard of proof is a preponderance of the evidence, which means marshaling enough evidence to show that the lawyer's position is *more likely than not* correct. Mental health professionals are rarely held to even the lowest legal standard of proof. Rightly so—the work is different. But mental health professionals perhaps sacrifice a thoroughness, a rigor, in not being challenged more often. A number of years ago one of us attended a clinical case conference in the midwest. A consultant was interviewing a patient who had been admitted to a psychiatric hospital for having jumped off a rather high bridge; despite the height of the bridge, the patient had suffered no injuries whatsoever. The discussion centered on the level of this patient's suicidality. As the case conference went on, one of the clinicians in attendance rather timidly asked whether there was any independent confirmation that this young woman had indeed jumped off the bridge. It turns out that there was not; she had shown up at an emergency room in soaking wet clothes and every clinician from that point on had simply taken her story at face value. The point is not that this young woman did—or did not—jump off the bridge, but rather that her treating clinicians did not know whether she had or hadn't, had not attempted to confirm whether she had or hadn't, and yet were proceeding as if this piece of her history were certain. Now clearly the clinical assessment would be quite different depending on whether this woman actually jumped off the bridge, or whether she *said* she jumped off the bridge, but did not. A little bit of lawyerly skepticism at the outset would, we think, have been useful for the treatment.

Lawyers apply this sort of skepticism all the time. They will ask how a clinician *knows* that a patient will hurt himself if released from the hospital, how a clinician *knows* that a particular treatment will work, or how a clinician *knows* that a patient cannot perform a certain job or task. While the manner in which the question is put may seem abrasive, insensitive, and not fully appreciative of the mental health professional's expertise, it is based on the legal model—at least a preponderance of the evidence, or 51% of the available data, must be the supporting foundation for any position, statement, or opinion.

Another thing to keep in mind is that a lawyer is a patient's (and, for that matter, a mental health professional's) legal representative. For a lawyer, representation means advocating for what the client *says* he wants—and therein lies the rub with mental health professionals. Clinicians are trained in the complexity of human behavior and see the oral expression of a desire as only one aspect of what the person really wants. Often mental health professionals will counsel an individual to delay acting until ample time has been devoted to exploring all the advantages and disadvantages of a particular course of action. Other times mental health professionals will press an individual to talk about feelings that are not verbally expressed. Thus the posture of the mental health professional—to delay and to explore—is often directly at odds with that of the lawyer—to act. This difference can be intensified by the lawyer's skepticism, in virtue of which the lawyer may discount reasons given by the mental health professional for caution and delay. Fallout includes the mental health professional feeling that her work and expertise are not valued, and frustrated that the lawyer is helping the patient accomplish what the mental health professional sees as not necessarily in the patient's best interests.

Despite these differences, there are many successful lawyer-clinician teams who do excellent work. If you are called upon to work with an attorney, try to keep three things in mind: First, both you and the lawyer are working on behalf of the client. While you may disagree about goals, each of you has been trained to assist your client. In that sense, each of you is working on the client's behalf. Second, find the time to ask yourself the sort of questions the lawyer would be interested in asking. Clinicians rarely engage in this sort of activity, in large part because they are rarely called upon to explain the rationale behind their treatment. Ask yourself questions like: What is my treatment plan? What facts in the history support my use of this plan? What facts in the history would be *in*consistent with this plan? Might there be other plans I have not considered that may be helpful? If I have made an intervention, such as an involuntary hospitalization, on what basis have I made that intervention? How certain am I that the intervention will be successful? On what facts or observations do I base my certainty? Try to place yourself in the shoes of the lawyer, and ask the skeptical questions she would ask. Third, find a time to sit with the lawyer to understand better what she is thinking about the case. Ask what the lawyer intends to do and why she intends to do it; explore the reasons behind her plan of action. Remember as you do so that the lawyer will hold your reasoning to a standard of evidence, so be prepared to explain the reasons behind *your* thinking as well. Above all, keep in mind that the more you and the lawyer can work *together*, the better each of you will serve your mutual client.

7. What is a deposition?

Depositions are part of a legal process called "discovery." Discovery is just that—a process whereby one party in a lawsuit discovers facts and information from another party in the lawsuit. The discovery process has several purposes: The facts and information garnered during discovery allow the parties to narrow and focus the issues at trial, facts and information that may be lost or forgotten before the trial actually takes place are recorded and thereby preserved, and the parties may be more disposed to settle the lawsuit after certain facts and information come to light. The process of discovery allows a party literally to discover the nature, strength, and weaknesses of the lawsuit it intends to bring. Depositions are an important part of the discovery process. Crucial to keep in mind is that, consistent with the purpose of discovery, the purpose of taking a deposition is for a party to learn *what it does not know.*

Depositions are particularly well-suited to uncovering unknown facts and information. The format is oral questions and oral responses. Questions can be asked on a wide range of topics, and the rules of admissibility—rules that can keep certain evidence out of a trial—are much less strict for depositions. Unlike what occurs at trial, a lawyer taking a deposition does not need to demonstrate that a particular question is relevant to the matter at hand. A wide berth is given to what may be asked. If an objection is raised to a particular question, the objection is noted and reviewed at trial. The question itself is answered.

Most depositions take place at the office of the attorney who wants the deposition—at a time all the parties agree on. Testimony at a deposition takes place under oath and a court stenographer is present to record the proceedings. A deposition may last from half an hour to several days, depending on the importance of the testimony being taken.

It is wise to consult your malpractice carrier any time you give testimony at a deposition, to see if the presence of a lawyer is indicated. If you receive a subpoena, be sure to check with your carrier and follow their advice on whether it is advisable for you to have legal representation. Two instances will require an attorney's presence: when the clinician is the defendant, that is, the person being sued, and when an issue of confidentiality or testimonial privilege is likely to arise. In the latter case, having a lawyer present is essential, insofar as answering a question may expose you to a claim that you breached your client's confidentiality (see chapter 7, Subpoenas and Court Orders).

8. Why is a deposition important?

The significance of a deposition cannot be overemphasized. Testimony is taken under oath, so false or misleading statements may lead to a charge of perjury. In addition, if what you say at trial is factually inconsistent with what you said at the deposition, your testimony at the deposition can be used to contradict—in legal parlance, "impeach"—you at trial. It is extremely useful to obtain a copy of the transcript following the deposition, for two reasons: First, you will want to check the transcript for accuracy and correct any mistakes for the final version; second, having a copy of the transcript will allow you to review what you said at the deposition before you testify at trial.

9. What are interrogatories?

Interrogatories are the *written* equivalent of a deposition. Interrogatories are sent only to the parties in the lawsuit, not to expert witnesses. When a party receives the interrogatories she will respond in writing and sign a sworn statement that the responses are true.

10. What is the difference between an expert witness and a fact witness?

A fact witness is an individual who has *personal knowledge* of some situation or event relevant to a legal proceeding. An expert witness need not have personal knowledge of the matter. Rather, an expert is called to testify because he has *special knowledge that can help the jury in making its decision.* While fact witnesses testify to *facts* of which they have direct knowledge, expert witnesses give *opinions* that derive from their unique expertise.

As an example, consider that one day you are walking down the aisle of the grocery store, slip on a banana peel, and aggravate that old knee injury to the point where you're unable to participate in the big croquet tournament this weekend. You sue the store for your injury. You will call as a *fact witness* anyone who was in the store and witnessed the events surrounding your accident: the baker who saw the banana on the floor immediately before you fell; the person at the cash register who saw you go down; the butcher who heard your bloodcurdling scream. All of these people have personal knowledge of what happened—they will testify as to the events that led to your injury based on what they saw and heard. Fact witnesses are allowed to testify *only* as to what they personally experienced. If they attempt to testify about matters of which they have no direct experience, the lawyer on the other side will become apoplectic and ask the judge to please tell the witness to stop speaking immediately.

You will call as an *expert witness* Dr. Peal, the world-famous authority in injuries suffered during banana falls. Dr. Peal did not see or hear you fall, but he has special knowledge having to do with how the knee turns in an unusual manner during a banana fall and the injuries unique to those dreadful contortions. Dr. Peal will testify about the severity of your injury, your likely prognosis, and your inability to participate in the up-coming croquet tournament. Note that Dr. Peal was not in the store when you fell, and he has no personal knowledge of what occurred. Rather, Dr. Peal's knowledge about your injury derives almost entirely from informa-tion he has received secondhand: your description of the fall, the X-rays, the report of the emergency room physician, and the reports submitted by your treating physician.

Two comments about expert witnesses. First, the expert is allowed to speak only on those matters his expertise covers. Dr. Peal will not be allowed to speak about the sorts of injuries that result from garbanzo bean falls, because he is only a banana fall expert. Garbanzo beans lie outside his area of expertise. Note how this restriction is somewhat like the restriction on fact witnesses, who are allowed to testify only as to matters of which they have personal knowledge. All witnesses—fact and expertise—may speak solely to those matters which lie within their direct experience (fact) or expertise (expert).

Second, the expert must testify as to the facts that underlie his expert opinion. Describing the facts upon which the expert opinion is based is called "laying the foundation." Dr. Peal, for example, will base his expert opinion—that you must wait one year before you play croquet again—on his examination of your knee, his review of your knee's medical record, and his exploration of the sprawling and sometimes treacherous croquet fields on which you compete. He will begin his testimony by describing in great detail his examination, his review, and his exploration. He will then say (in an appropriately ponderous tone), "Based on these facts, I am of the opinion that . . . " Dr. Peal has laid his foundation.

11. How is it decided who will be an expert witness?
The judge decides who will be "qualified" as an expert witness. Judges have a great deal of discretion in this regard; there isn't any list of experts, or any list of specific qualifications. Rather, the trial judge asks two ques-tions: Does the expert know things the jury most likely does not? Will the expert's knowledge help the jury make its decision? If the answer to both questions is "yes," the trial judge is free to qualify the person as an expert and allow him to give expert opinions at trial.

12. If I receive a subpoena and must testify at a deposition about a therapy case, am I an expert witness or a fact witness?

You can be subpoenaed as either, so *be clear about whether you are being called to testify as an expert or as a fact witness.* Important to keep in mind is that a lawyer will not usually send a subpoena to his own witness; if you do receive a subpoena, then, it is likely from the *other* side. Now a lawyer would subpoena you as an expert only if you had already been identified as an expert by *your* side—so if you receive a subpoena and are confused about whether you are an expert or a fact witness, you are almost certainly a fact witness.

13. What should I know if I am called to testify as a fact witness?

The following five points may be helpful.

First, you are not required to spend time preparing for the deposition, either by reading your notes or reviewing the therapy. Preparing may lessen your anxiety, but time so spent will not be compensated. If you do decide to prepare, it's on your own time.

Second, should you decide to prepare, know that any documents you make regarding your patient's treatment—including "personal" notes made in contemplation of your testimony at the deposition—are subject to a subpoena! To make matters even worse, an attorney can question you about *conversations* you held in preparation for the deposition, with whomever, including your patient and your patient's attorney. The sole exception is that you do not have to answer questions about conversations you had with your own attorney.

Third, make your answers responsive to the questions. Volunteer nothing and speculate even less. "I don't recall" or "I don't know" are fine answers, if true. Keep in mind that a deposition is neither an intelligence test nor a memory competition. Attempts to impress the opposing attorney with your memory may be suddenly upended at trial, when written documents show exactly the opposite of what you testified under oath at the deposition.

Fourth, although you are being called as a fact witness, the opposing attorney will very likely ask you to give an expert opinion. If you are asked a question that demands *more than your personal knowledge of this treatment and this patient,* give your attorney time to object before beginning your answer. If, for example, you are asked to explain the usual prognosis for patients with this diagnosis, to discuss the controversy surrounding what medication should be given to such patients, or to weigh in on the debate over the treatment of choice, you are being asked to provide expert testimony, testimony that is not grounded in your knowledge of this particular treatment and this particular patient. Your attorney may object and, if so, your testimony will be limited to the facts of which you are personally aware.

Finally, you must have written permission from your patient or an order from the court (see chapter 7, Subpoenas and Court Orders) before you disclose any information or release any records. Only your patient's written permission or an order from the court will allow you to disclose information that is confidential or protected by testimonial privilege. A subpoena alone will not suffice.

14. Does whether I am an expert witness or a fact witness make any difference in how much I am paid?

Whether you are a fact or an expert witness makes an *enormous* difference in how much you are paid. *Expert witnesses* generally charge an hourly fee for their services, which may consist of interviewing the patient, reviewing the record, speaking with current or former treaters, discussing the case with lawyers, and traveling to and from where the testimony is taken. An expert witness who is subpoenaed by the opposition lawyer will be paid by the opposition; this arrangement should be made before the expert testifies.

Fact witnesses are paid a fee established by statute. The fee in Massachusetts is $6 per day (no, that's not a typo—$6 per *day*), a bit more should they have to travel any distance. That said, clinicians who are called as fact witnesses may attempt to negotiate a reasonable hourly fee—usually through an attorney—for time spent at the deposition, and any time spent in preparation for the deposition. Both sides have an incentive to negotiate in these circumstances. The clinician testifying would obviously like to get paid more than a few dollars, especially since she will almost certainly have to cancel patients. The attorney who has issued the subpoena does not want a clinician who is angry at having to cancel patients, frustrated about such meager pay, and eager to say as little as possible in order to get back to the office. Often the negotiated payment is the clinician's hourly treatment fee.

15. What is a statute of limitations?

The law seeks to promote justice. If one individual injures another, justice requires that the injured party be allowed to seek compensation for that injury. The question then arises: How long should the injured party be able to wait before she brings a lawsuit? Some might say "as long as she likes"; after all, why add insult to the injury by limiting options regarding when she may sue?

The law takes a different position. The law limits the amount of time that may pass before you bring a suit, for two reasons. First, even though someone did injure you, there comes a point in time when that person should be able to get on with his life, without fear of being brought into court. Such a limitation allows people to go about the business of their lives without worrying that events from long ago could come back to burden them. A rule that limits the amount of time injured parties have to bring lawsuits thus promotes efficiency. Second, evidence becomes stale with time. A lawsuit provides you the opportunity to show that another person injured you; that person has the opportunity, in turn, to defend himself. If too great a time passes before you file the suit, the person's ability to defend himself proportionately diminishes—memories fade, physical evidence deteriorates, and people helpful to a defense become old and die. For these reasons, the law imposes a limit: A lawsuit must be brought within a specified period of time following an injury. If a longer period of time passes, the lawsuit will not be heard. The *statute of limitations* specifies the length of this time period.

16. What is the statute of limitations for malpractice lawsuits in Massachusetts?

M.G.L. chapter 260, section 2A states, "Actions of tort . . . to recover for personal injuries . . . shall be commenced only within three years after the cause of action accrues." Thus, in Massachusetts, the statute of limitations for a malpractice lawsuit is three years. (See questions 18 and 19 for exceptions to the Massachusetts statute of limitations.)

17. Do licensing boards have statutes of limitations?

The Board of Registration in Medicine has a six-year statute of limitations. The six-year statute applies in all cases, except where the Board feels it should be extended for good cause. The Boards of Registration in Psychology, Social Work, and Allied Mental Health have no official statutes of limitations. These Boards may, however, consider a combination of the length of time that has passed and the seriousness of the complaint when deciding whether to allow a complaint to go forward. If not terribly serious, for example, a Board may dismiss a complaint based on an action that took place a substantial time ago (e.g., 10 years).

Professional associations do have statutes of limitations. The National Association of Social Workers, for example, requires that an ethics complaint be filed within one year of the event. The Ethics Committee of the American Psychological Association will consider a complaint filed by a member of the APA within one year of when the event occurred or was discovered; nonmembers have five years to file. Special circumstances can extend the APA's statute of limitations.

18. What is the discovery rule?

The Massachusetts statute of limitations gives an individual three years from the time of an injury to file a lawsuit in court. The discovery rule applies when an individual does not realize that she has been harmed or, although realizing that she has been harmed, does not realize that a particular treater was the cause of her harm. Massachusetts courts have reasoned that in such cases it would violate "fundamental fairness" for the statute of limitations to begin counting at the moment the injury occurs. The discovery rule says that the three-year statute of limitations begins counting only when a patient knows, or reasonably should know, that she has been harmed by her treater.

In *Riley v. Presnell* (409 Mass. 239, 1991), the SJC applied the discovery rule to a case in which a therapist had sexually abused a patient. The facts were as follows:

> In 1975, the plaintiff, Robert Scott Riley, was referred to the defendant, Dr. Walter M. Presnell, by the Massachusetts Rehabilitation Commission. Riley was an epileptic who had been experiencing some emotional difficulties, but did not suffer from any major psychopathology at the time he began treatment. Some months into therapy, Dr. Presnell began to introduce alcohol and marijuana into the therapy sessions. The use of these substances continued and increased through the four years of therapy. Dr. Presnell also dispensed liberal prescriptions of Valium to Riley. On at least two occasions, purportedly as a way to deal with Riley's feelings toward his father, Dr. Presnell persuaded Riley to engage in various sexual acts with him. . . . Dr. Presnell told Riley not to tell anyone of the nature of the therapy because it was "special" and the world would neither understand nor approve. (241)

Dr. Presnell's "treatment" was discovered when Mr. Riley began treatment with another therapist, by which time Mr. Riley was addicted to

Valium, "experiencing more severe emotional and psychological problems, . . . drinking heavily, and [having] domestic problems" (241). Mr. Riley decided to sue Dr. Presnell. The problem was that the suit was filed nearly 10 years after the injury had occurred, or seven years after the statute of limitations had run out.

The SJC reasoned that while Mr. Riley certainly knew that he was suffering from a variety of ailments, he did not discover *that Dr. Presnell was the cause of those ailments* until he began working with another therapist. The SJC stated that it would hardly be fair for Dr. Presnell to go free simply because the statute of limitations had passed. The SJC therefore applied the discovery rule.

In deciding when Mr. Riley "knew, or reasonably should have known," that Dr. Presnell was the cause of his ailments, the SJC looked to the "reasonable person" standard. According to the reasonable person standard, the court asks when a reasonable person who had undergone such an experience would know that he had been injured by the conduct in question. From *that* point in time Mr. Riley had three years to file his lawsuit against Dr. Presnell.

19. How do the statute of limitations and the discovery rule apply to cases involving minors?

In general, the statute of limitations does not begin to run until a minor reaches the age of majority. Thus, a minor has three years from her 18th birthday, or until the age of 21, before the statute of limitations would prevent her from bringing a lawsuit.

Massachusetts has a statute that applies the discovery rule to cases involving the sexual abuse of a minor. The statute, M.G.L. chapter 260, section 4C, titled "Sexual Abuse of Minors," first states the rule that an individual has three years from her 18th birthday, or until the age of 21, until the statute of limitations would prevent her from filing a lawsuit. Section 4C then states that the individual must file the lawsuit "within three years of the time the victim discovered or *reasonably should have discovered* [italics added] that an emotional or psychological injury or condition" was caused by the perpetrator.

When would a "reasonable person" discover that an injury, perhaps a psychological symptom such as nightmares, flashbacks, or the inability to enjoy sex, was caused by a perpetrator's sexual abuse? The SJC held that one should ask "what is expected of a reasonable and ordinary person *under similar traumatic circumstances* [italics added]" (*Phinney v.*

Morgan, 39 Mass. App. Ct. 202 [1995; at 206]). So, for example, take a "reasonable and ordinary" young woman who had been sexually abused during childhood, and ask when she would come to realize that her symptoms were caused by the sexual abuse. Might such a "reasonable and ordinary" young woman take longer than the statutory three years to draw a connection between her symptoms and the sexual abuse? No doubt. And the SJC has said as much:

> We recognize that because of the nature of the injury and the relationship of the parties, a child may repress all memory of the abuse, lack understanding of the wrongfulness of the conduct, or be unaware of any harm or its cause until years after the abuse. . . . Accordingly, the very same factors that have prompted the application of the discovery rule to other [harmful] conduct support its application to tort claims arising out of incestuous child abuse . . . Those factors are an unawareness that the defendant committed a wrongful act at the time of its commission; the plaintiff's trust in the defendant; the defendant's control over the facts giving rise to the plaintiff's cause of action; and the necessity of a triggering event which makes the plaintiff aware of the defendant's potential liability. (*Phinney* at 204–205)

A court should take all of these factors into consideration in determining when a "reasonable and ordinary" person who had been sexually abused during childhood would come to realize that her symptoms had been caused by the perpetrator of the sexual abuse. Only then does the three-year statute of limitations begin to run.

20. What is the Medical Malpractice Tribunal?
The Medical Malpractice Tribunal (established by M.G.L. chapter 231, section 60B) serves as a screening mechanism for malpractice cases. The Tribunal consists of three people (hence a "tribunal"): a judge, an attorney, and a person from the discipline in which the injury occurred. The individual who claims to have been injured (the plaintiff) presents evidence to the Tribunal, which must decide whether the case raises "a legitimate question of liability" or "is merely an unfortunate medical result." To show that the case raises a legitimate question of liability, the plaintiff must present at least some evidence on each of the four "Ds" (see chapter 2). If the Tribunal decides in the plaintiff's favor, the case goes to trial. If the Tribunal decides against the plaintiff, the case stops, unless the plaintiff posts a bond within 30 days. The bond is $6000, although the judge

on the Tribunal can raise or lower this amount under appropriate circumstances.

21. What is the Americans with Disabilities Act?

The Americans with Disabilities Act, signed by President Bush in 1990, provides sweeping federal protection for individuals with disabilities, including mental disabilities, in areas of employment, public services, and private services that accommodate the public. To be eligible for protection under the Act, an individual must have an impairment, a record of an impairment, or be regarded as having an impairment that substantially limits one or more major life activities. Thus, it targets both individuals who have an impairment that keeps them out of the mainstream of their community's social and economic life, and individuals who, because of stereotypes, may be kept out of the mainstream of their community's social and economic life.

Under the Americans with Disabilities Act, an employer may not refuse to hire and may not fire an individual because of a disability if that individual can perform the "essential functions" of the job, either with or without "reasonable accommodation." The essential functions are those duties that are necessary to the task; it would be necessary for an individual working as a hotel receptionist, for example, to interact with hotel guests. A reasonable accommodation is a modification that allows the individual to perform the essential functions of the job. A person with a mental disability, for example, may need time during working hours to see a therapist; such time would be a reasonable accommodation. A more severe mental disability may require several days off for a brief inpatient stay; additional unpaid leave for the purpose of a hospitalization could also be considered a reasonable accommodation.

5

CIVIL COMMITMENT

Civil commitment refers to the process by which the state deprives an individual of his civil liberties because a risk of harm arises from mental illness. The term "civil" distinguishes this sort of commitment from a criminal commitment, that is, a commitment that follows a finding of guilt in a criminal court of law. In the criminal context, a constitutional safeguard called "due process" comes into play. Due process requires that, before we deprive an individual of his liberty, by placing him in jail, for example, we ensure that he is apprised of his rights, allowed representation by a lawyer, given a fair trial, and the like. In civil commitment we dispense with some of these safeguards. We do so because the state is endowed with two sorts of power: the _parens patriae power_, the authority to act like a parent and care for a citizen who is not able to care for himself, and the _police power_, the authority to detain an individual who is a danger to himself or to someone else.

For many years in this country, mental illness alone was enough to justify depriving an individual of his liberty. Thus, were an individual simply "in need of treatment," he could be placed against his will in a psychiatric hospital. Times have changed, however, and today an individual's mental illness must present an issue of safety before he may be civilly committed to a psychiatric hospital.

QUESTIONS DISCUSSED IN THIS CHAPTER

22. Where are the laws and regulations that govern psychiatric hospitalizations?
23. What is the standard for civil commitment in Massachusetts?
24. Which court has jurisdiction over civil commitment cases?
25. What is the standard of proof in civil commitment cases?
26. How long does a civil commitment last?
27. Under chapter 123, who actually commits the patient?
28. The law says that a person must be mentally ill before he can be committed to a hospital. Does the law define mental illness?
29. What is a conditional voluntary admission?
30. What is a three-day paper?
31. What is a pink paper?
32. The question above said that the pink paper was good for 10 days; before that a three-day paper was mentioned. How do these different times fit together?
33. You've talked about civil commitment in terms of mental illness. Can alcohol and other substances provide the basis for an involuntary hospitalization?
34. What rights does a psychiatric inpatient have?
35. Do psychiatric patients have the right to refuse antipsychotic medication?
36. May restraints and seclusion be used for therapeutic purposes?
37. Chapter 123 gives a great deal of authority to mental health professionals. Could a patient who had been involuntarily sent to a hospital with a pink paper, involuntarily admitted to a psychiatric unit, or unwillingly placed in restraints, ever have cause to sue?
38. How should I handle a situation in which a client, who clearly meets commitment criteria, begins to get up and walk out of my office? Should I ever attempt physically to restrain a client?
39. Does Massachusetts have a law providing for outpatient commitment?

> ## NOTE TO OUR READERS
>
> The law lives and breathes; as circumstances change, the law changes as well. At this book's publication, the Massachusetts legislature was considering altering certain aspects of chapter 123. It is likely, for example, that the length of time a patient may be involuntarily hospitalized under section 12 would be reduced. It is also likely that a patient will be entitled to a hearing on a petition for commitment within a shorter period of time than currently provided for by chapter 123. As you read questions 29, 31, and 32, keep these likely changes in mind. Your profession's newsletter, as well as the popular press, will certainly note and discuss these changes.

DISCUSSION

22. Where are the laws and regulations that govern psychiatric hospitalizations?

The laws governing psychiatric hospitalizations are found in chapter 123 of the Massachusetts General Laws. Chapter 123, "Mental Health," covers a wide range of topics, from defining "licensed mental health professional" all the way to describing the duties of the Commissioner of Mental Health. The heart of chapter 123 consists of the rules that govern the treatment of individuals suffering from serious mental illness.

Chapter 123 provides that the Department of Mental Health may write regulations as a way of carrying out its responsibilities. These regulations are found in the Code of Massachusetts Regulations, chapter 104. If you have a question about the Department of Mental Health or about psychiatric hospitalizations, the first place to look will therefore be the M.G.L., chapter 123, or the CMR, chapter 104.

Happy hunting.

23. What is the standard for civil commitment in Massachusetts?

Sections 1, 7, and 8 of M.G.L. chapter 123 lay out the circumstances under which an individual may be involuntarily placed in a psychiatric hospital. Sections 7 and 8 have two requirements for civil commitment: (1) the individual must be mentally ill; and (2) failure to hospitalize the individual (section 7), or discharge from the hospital (section 8), would "create a likelihood of serious harm."* Section 1 defines "likelihood of serious harm" as:

> (1) a substantial risk of physical harm to the person himself as manifested by evidence of, threats of, or attempts at, suicide or serious bodily harm; (2) a substantial risk of physical harm to other persons as manifested by evidence of homicidal or other violent behavior or evidence that others are placed in reasonable fear of violent behavior and serious physical harm to them; or (3) a very substantial risk of physical impairment or injury to the person himself as manifested by evidence that such person's judgment is so affected that he is unable to protect himself in the community and that reasonable provision for his protection is not available in the community.

Note three things about section 1 of chapter 123. First, the provision defines the likelihood of *serious* harm. Thus, the provision only applies when the threatened harm is serious, that is, not trivial. Second, the likelihood of the harm must consist of a *substantial* risk of physical harm to the person himself, a *substantial* risk of physical harm to others, or a *very substantial* risk of physical impairment or injury to the person himself. Third, the substantial or very substantial risk must be supported *by specific evidence*. This standard is a far cry from the former "in need of treatment" standard.

One last point: An individual may be civilly committed to a psychiatric hospital *only when no less restrictive setting would suffice to attenuate the risk.*

24. Which court has jurisdiction over civil commitment cases?

Chapter 123, sections 7 and 8 give the district court and the juvenile court jurisdiction over civil commitment cases.

---

* M.G.L. 123, section 7 states that the superintendent of a hospital may petition the court to commit an individual if "failure to hospitalize would create a likelihood of serious harm" by reason of mental illness. The following section of chapter 123, section 8, states that, at the commitment hearing, the court will determine whether discharging the individual from the hospital would "create a likelihood of serious harm" by reason of mental illness. The import of sections 7 and 8 is that the grounds for a petition to commit, and the grounds for a commitment, are the same: If not in the hospital, an individual would create a likelihood of serious harm by reason of mental illness.

CIVIL COMMITMENT

M.G.L. c.123, §§1, 7, and 8

I.   Individual is **mentally ill** (§§7 and 8).

II. Failure to hospitalize or discharge from the hospital creates **"likelihood of serious harm"** (§§7 and 8)

III. Likelihood of serious harm defined as (§1):
   A. Substantial risk of physical harm to person himself.
   B. Substantial risk of physical harm to other persons.
   C. Very substantial risk of physical impairment or injury to the person himself.

IV. Substantial or very substantial risk must be supported **by specific evidence** (§1).
   A. Risk of harm to self supported by evidence of threats of or attempts at:
      1. Suicide.
      2. Serious bodily harm.
   B. Risk of harm to others supported by evidence of:
      1. Homicidal or other violent behavior.
      2. Others are placed in reasonable fear of violent behavior and serious physical harm.
   C. Risk of physical impairment or injury to the person himself supported by evidence of:
      1. Inability to protect himself in the community due to impairment in judgment and;
      2. Reasonable provision for his protection not available in the community.

V.   **No setting less restrictive** than the hospital would suffice to attenuate the risk.

25. What is the standard of proof in civil commitment cases?

In *Superintendent of Worcester State Hospital v. Laura Hagberg,* 374 Mass. 271 (1978), the SJC held that a civil commitment hearing involves a matter of great importance. When an individual is committed to a psychiatric hospital, that individual suffers a *loss of liberty* and undergoes *the stigma attached to mental illness.* The SJC reasoned that the loss of liberty and the stigma attached to mental illness require a standard of proof equivalent to the standard of proof required in a criminal proceeding, where the defendant's liberty is at stake. That standard is proof *beyond a reasonable doubt.* Thus, in a civil commitment hearing, the individual bringing the petition—most often the superintendent of a hospital—must show beyond a reasonable doubt that the individual creates a risk by reason of mental illness. Put in the language of the statute, the superintendent must show beyond a reasonable doubt that discharge from the hospital would create a likelihood of serious harm.

26. How long does a civil commitment last?
Section 8 of chapter 123 states that the initial commitment lasts for up to six months. Commitments following the initial commitment are for a period up to one year.

27. Under chapter 123, who actually commits the patient?
This point is extremely important. Only a *judge* has the authority to commit an individual to a psychiatric hospital. Although licensed psychiatrists, qualified* psychologists, qualified psychiatric nurses, and police officers may have an individual transported to a psychiatric hospital against that individual's will, and psychiatrists may admit an individual involuntarily to a psychiatric unit for up to 10 days under section 12, only a judge may order a civil commitment. The authority vested in psychiatrists under section 12 is really nothing other than the authority to provide for a period of time to stabilize or assess a patient. When it comes to ordering a change in legal status, whether the change comes in the form of a civil commitment or a declaration of incompetence, the power and authority rest only in a judge.

The sole exception arises when a guardian has been appointed under chapter 201, section 6, and the judge has specifically authorized the guardian to admit or commit the ward to a psychiatric hospital (see chapter 8, Guardians, Conservators, and Substitute Decision-Making).

28. The law says that a person must be mentally ill before he can be committed to a hospital. Does the law define mental illness?
104 CMR 27.05 defines mental illness as "a substantial disorder of thought, mood, perception, orientation, or memory which grossly impairs judg-

---

* A mental health professional who has been "qualified" has received a special designation by the Commonwealth to perform certain functions, such as filling out a "pink paper," also known as a "section 12" (see question 31). Chapter 123, section 1 and 104 CMR 33.02 explain what makes psychologists and psychiatric nurses "qualified."

MENTAL ILLNESS FOR PURPOSES OF CIVIL COMMITMENT

104 CMR 27.05

I. Disorder must be **substantial**.

II. Disorder must affect (at least one of the following):
   A. Thought
   B. Mood
   C. Perception
   D. Orientation
   E. Memory

III. Disorder must **grossly** impair (at least one of the following):
   A. Judgment
   B. Behavior
   C. Capacity to recognize reality
   D. Ability to meet ordinary demands of life

IV. "Mental illness" does **not** include alcoholism or substance abuse.

---

ment, behavior, capacity to recognize reality or ability to meet the ordinary demands of life." Note how the definition emphasizes the severity of the illness: The disorder must be "substantial"; the ego functions "grossly" impaired. *104 CMR 27.05 is not talking about the worried well.* Note also how the definition speaks to functional abilities. The disorder must impair those capacities that allow us to go about our daily lives: the capacity to make judgments, to behave in an appropriate manner, to recognize the world around us, and to take care of the normal sorts of things we need to take care of as we make our way through the day. Finally, further on, 104 CMR 27.05 states that the definition of mental illness does not include alcoholism or substance abuse.

29. What is a conditional voluntary admission?

Section 10 of chapter 123 provides that any individual may voluntarily sign himself into a hospital, provided the individual is in need of treatment and the hospital is an appropriate setting. Section 11 says that a person who signs himself into the hospital under section 10 "shall be free to leave . . . at any time," except that "the superintendent may restrict the right to leave or withdraw to normal working hours and weekdays and, in his discretion, may require persons . . . to give three days written notice of their intention to leave or withdraw." *The requirement of giving three days notice before leaving is the condition upon which the individual enters the hospital.* Note that this provision is not mandatory; the treaters may decide that the person is fine and can leave immediately. What the condition does is to vest the superintendent of the hospital with the authority to say, "This person is not well enough to leave, and I will now request that a court order an *involuntary* hospitalization." If the superintendent petitions for civil commitment, the individual remains at the hospital until the commitment hearing is held. Commitment hearings must be held within 14 days of when the petition is filed.

30. What is a three-day paper?
A three-day paper is a notice issued by a conditional voluntary patient that he intends to leave the hospital. The three-day period of time comes from the requirement that a patient give three days notice of his intention to leave the hospital. When a patient signs a three-day paper, the hospital may petition for a commitment or choose simply to allow the three days to pass without doing anything, in which case the individual is discharged no later than three days after he signed the paper. Again, notice the conditional quality of the admission.

31. What is a pink paper?
A "pink paper" (it really is a pink sheet of paper), otherwise known as a "section 12"—from section 12 of chapter 123, is the mechanism by which one moves to hospitalize an individual believed to meet the criteria for civil commitment. Section 12 has a number of provisions; we will comment on four.

First, section 12 provides that a licensed physician, qualified psychologist, qualified psychiatric nurse mental health clinical specialist or, if none of these people is available and the situation is an emergency, a police officer, may order that a mentally ill individual be restrained and taken to a hospital. The psychiatrist, psychologist, nurse, or police officer must have reason to believe that failure to hospitalize would create a likelihood of serious harm by reason of mental illness. Section 12 makes clear that whoever has issued the order to restrain and transport should tell the hospital what's going on and whether continued restraints are likely to be necessary.

Second, section 12 provides that an individual who is restrained and brought to the hospital may be admitted *only if a designated physician has signed the pink paper.* If the order to restrain and transport has been filled out by someone other than a designated physician, a designated physician must examine the individual prior to admission, to determine whether failure to hospitalize the individual would create a likelihood of serious harm by reason of mental illness.

Third, an admission under section 12 is for 10 days. The hospital must decide, within those 10 days, whether to petition to commit the patient or to discharge the patient. If the hospital makes no decision—does nothing—the patient will be discharged no later than 10 days after admission, unless he signs into the hospital on a conditional voluntary basis. The individual must be told that hospitalization pursuant to section 12 cannot exceed 10 days. Also, before a person is admitted by a pink paper, he must be given the opportunity to apply for a conditional voluntary admission. *The law and public policy favor the least restrictive means of hospitalization. Because a conditional voluntary admission is seen as less restrictive than an involuntary admission, the law will authorize an involuntary hospitalization only when an individual meets commitment criteria and will not agree to a conditional voluntary hospitalization.* Consistent with the law's preference for voluntary, rather than involuntary, admissions, 104 CMR 27.08 provides that an individual may sign in as a conditional voluntary patient at any point during the 10-day period he has been hospitalized pursuant to a pink paper.

Fourth, section 12 states that "any person" may apply to the appropriate court in order to hospitalize an individual believed to meet commitment criteria. If the judge, after hearing the evidence, agrees that the person may need to be committed, he may issue a warrant and have the individual apprehended and then examined by a physician or a qualified psychologist. If the examination indicates that failure to hospitalize the individual would create a likelihood of serious harm, the judge may order the person committed for up to 10 days.

32. The question above said that the pink paper was good for 10 days; before that a three-day paper was mentioned. How do these different times fit together?

Let's start with the principle that the law favors the least restrictive means of hospitalization. The pink paper, or section 12 as it is also known, is an application to hospitalize someone who meets commitment criteria. Yet, as we learned above, even a person meeting commitment criteria must first be given the opportunity to apply for a conditional voluntary admission.

Consider Phil, a middle-aged man with a lengthy history of work in the health professions. A victim of late onset schizophrenia, Phil now lives in a supported housing unit and spends most of his days in a sheltered work setting or, when short on cash, wandering the streets picking up cans and bottles. Occasionally Phil will become agitated and delusional. He's a large man and, while he's never actually assaulted anyone, can be quite threatening. One day, during an episode of acute psychosis, Phil comes to believe that a small neighborhood store has been invaded by aliens. He becomes quite agitated, to the point of throwing a garbage can through the storefront window. The police, who manage to subdue Phil, take him to the nearest emergency room of a hospital with a psychiatric unit. There, the psychiatrist on call decides that Phil meets criteria for civil commitment.

Let's now consider three scenarios. In the first scenario, the examining psychiatrist tells Phil how concerned she is about his safety and how someone could easily have gotten hurt, perhaps badly, back at the store. Phil, having been given enough medication to calm down somewhat, agrees that he is not ready to go home. He signs into the hospital as a conditional voluntary patient. He remains at the hospital and receives treatment until both he and his therapist feel he is ready to leave. On a mutually agreed upon date, Phil is discharged back into the community and returns to his group home.

In the second scenario, Phil tells the examining psychiatrist that he is absolutely fine and that "the hospital people" aren't understanding "the danger everyone is in." Phil will not agree to sign into the hospital on a conditional voluntary basis, and insists on being released immediately. In this instance, section 12 gives the hospital the authority to keep Phil for up to 10 days, during which time the treaters will decide whether to petition the court for further commitment. The hospital signs the section 12, and chooses to wait a few days to see whether Phil's mental status changes. Since no significant changes are forthcoming, the hospital files a petition for commitment within 10 days and asks the judge to commit Phil. If the judge grants this request, Phil is then an involuntary patient at the hospital. Note that if the hospital did nothing in this 10-day period, Phil would be released no later than 10 days after the admission. Put another way, when it comes to a section 12, not to decide is to decide. If the hospital doesn't do anything in the 10-day period, the patient is discharged.

In the third scenario, Phil agrees with the emergency room physician that he is not ready to leave the hospital. He says that he'll stay and signs a conditional voluntary admission. After two weeks Phil begins to get restless and insists that he is ready to go. The treatment team, feeling that the vestiges of Phil's delusion about an alien invasion are still present and active, refuses to release Phil back into the community. Phil submits a three-day paper, thereby serving the team notice that he intends to leave the hospital no later than three days hence. The team must then decide whether Phil continues to meet commitment criteria or whether, while they would prefer his treatment to continue on an inpatient basis, he does not meet commitment criteria and must be released. The team has three days to make its decision. If the team feels that Phil meets commitment criteria, it will file a petition for commitment within the three-day period. Phil will remain at the hospital until the commitment hearing is held. If the team decides not to petition for commitment, the hospital will discharge Phil no later than the third day after he signed the paper.

33. You've talked about civil commitment in terms of mental illness. Can alcohol and other substances provide the basis for an involuntary hospitalization?

Section 35 of chapter 123 defines an alcoholic or substance abuser as someone who has "lost control" over his use of substances, or someone whose substance use "substantially injures his health or substantially interferes with his social or economic functioning." If either of these conditions is present, the individual meets the definition of an alcoholic or substance abuser; at that point, section 35 allows any one of a number of individuals, including a spouse, relative, or physician, to ask a court to commit that individual. Section 35 provides that, in response to such a request, the court will "immediately" schedule a hearing and may have the individual arrested if he does not appear.

The judge commits an individual under section 35 if "there is a likelihood of serious harm as the result of his alcoholism or substance abuse." As defined in section 1 of chapter 123, "likelihood of serious harm" means "substantial risk of physical harm to the person himself," "substantial risk of physical harm to other persons," or "very substantial risk of physical impairment or injury to the person himself." Thus, as sections 7 and 8 tie *mental illness* to harm, impairment, or injury, to form the basis for civil commitment, so section 35 ties *alcoholism or substance abuse* to harm, impairment, or injury to form the basis for civil commitment. When a person speaks of a "section 35," then, at issue is a civil commitment based on alcohol or substance abuse. A section 35 commitment lasts no longer than 30 days, although the individual may be released sooner, if release does not entail the "likelihood of serious harm."

Two final notes about section 35. First, individuals committed for abusing alcohol or other substances may be sent to Bridgewater or Framingham (depending on their gender) if they are in need of strict security. Otherwise, individuals may be sent to a program approved by the Department of Public Health. Once there, however, the individual must be "housed and treated separately from convicted criminals." Thus, section 35 is explicit that the purpose of commitment under this section is treatment, not punishment. Second, there is no "pink paper" for alcoholics or substance abusers.

34. What rights does a psychiatric inpatient have?

Chapter 123, sections 23 and 24, and 104 CMR 27.14 enumerate civil rights that cannot be denied individuals admitted to a psychiatric hospital. Among others, these rights include the right to marry, make a will, vote, buy or sell property, and the catchall, "to manage one's affairs." Note that an individual can be deprived of certain rights if judged to be incompetent. Admission to a psychiatric hospital, however, in and of itself, does not render an individual incompetent. Quite the contrary—the law says explicitly that these rights remain intact following admission.

Rights accorded to psychiatric patients include the right to send unopened letters to the Governor, the Commissioner of the Department of Mental Health, a doctor, a lawyer, a family member, a member of the clergy, and a court, on stationery and with postage provided by the hospital. The physician, lawyer, or clergy must be allowed to visit at any reasonable time; letters to, and visits by, other individuals may be denied only if the hospital superintendent determines that the letters or visits are not in the patient's best interests. In addition, patients must be allowed to wear their own clothes, to have a reasonable sum of money to spend on "canteen expenses and small purchases," to have a private storage place for personal effects, and to make confidential telephone calls. Patients also have the right to refuse ECT, psychosurgery, and antipsychotic medication (see the following question for further discussion of the right to refuse antipsychotic medication).

104 CMR 27.14 and 27.15 have a number of mechanisms to ensure that these rights are protected. First, each patient is given a list of these rights upon admission; second, each hospital must have a copy of these rights posted in a conspicuous place; third, hospitals must appoint a human rights officer; and fourth, each DMH hospital must have a human rights committee.

35. Do psychiatric patients have the right to refuse antipsychotic medication?

The right to refuse medication has a long and illustrious history in the Commonwealth of Massachusetts. It was in this Commonwealth that two well-known cases involving the right to refuse, *Superintendent of Belchertown State School v. Saikewicz*, 373 Mass. 728 (1977), and *Rogers v. Commissioner of the Department of Mental Health*, 390 Mass. 489 (1983), were decided. In *Saikewicz*, the SJC was faced with the question of whether to allow a 67-year-old man with a mental age of slightly under 3 years to forego chemotherapy for leukemia. The Court termed chemotherapy in this case a "life-prolonging medical treatment," insofar as the chemotherapy could treat, as opposed to cure, the leukemia. The Court explained that the state had four interests that would argue in favor of providing medical treatment in such a life-threatening situation: (1) preserving life, (2) preventing suicide, (3) protecting the ethical integrity of the medical profession, and (4) protecting innocent third parties. The SJC weighed these interests against Mr. Saikewicz's right to refuse treatment. The Court was unequivocal in its reasoning that:

> The constitutional right to privacy, as we conceive it, is an expression of the sanctity of individual free choice and self-determination as fundamental constituents of life. The value of life as so perceived is lessened not by a decision to refuse treatment, but by the failure to allow a competent human being the right of choice. (Saikewicz at 742; footnote omitted)

The Court concluded that "no state interest [is] sufficient to counterbalance a patient's decision to decline life-prolonging medical treatment . . . [so that] the patient's right to privacy and self-determination is entitled to enforcement" (*Saikewicz* at 759). Mr. Saikewicz, through his guardian, was permitted to exercise his right to refuse treatment.

In *Rogers*, the Court addressed the question of an involuntarily committed psychiatric patient's right to refuse antipsychotic medication. The Court emphasized the great weight given to a patient's right to make treatment decisions:

> The doctor must offer treatment to the involuntarily committed patient, but, since it is the patient who bears the risks as well as the benefits of treatment by antipsychotic drugs, and must suffer the consequences of any treatment decision, the patient has the right to make that decision. In short, treatment decisions are the patient's prerogative solely. (*Rogers* at 501)

In a footnote to this passage, the Court reemphasized the point that treatment decisions belong to the patient, regardless of the consequences:

> Even if the patient's choice will not achieve the restoration of the patient's health, or will result in longer hospitalization, that choice must be respected. *The patient has the right to be wrong in the choice of treatment* [italics added]. (*Rogers* at 501)

The SJC then applied this analysis to the case of an individual who had been involuntarily committed to a psychiatric hospital. The Court concluded that antipsychotic medication may be administered to an unwilling patient only "in order to avoid the 'immediate, substantial, and irreversible deterioration of a serious mental illness'" (*Rogers* at 521, quoting *Guardianship of Roe,* 383 Mass. 415, at 441 [1981]). If the treaters determine that the antipsychotic medication should continue, yet the individual objects, the treaters must go to court and ask a judge to declare the patient incompetent. If the individual is deemed incompetent by the court, the judge should decide what to do by making a "substituted judgment treatment plan determination" (*Rogers* at 512). Under this standard, the judge will decide what the individual *would decide if competent*; this decision may be either to accept, or to refuse, the antipsychotic medication.

A very clear theme runs through decisions of the Massachusetts Supreme Judicial Court: Individuals have the right to refuse medical treatment. While this right is not absolute, it has been given great weight, even when balanced against the four relevant state interests: to preserve life, to prevent suicide, to protect the interests of innocent third parties, and to preserve the ethical integrity of the medical profession. The right to refuse treatment extends to incompetent individuals; indeed, the right of incompetent individuals to refuse treatment, though expressed through a guardian, is the same as that of competent individuals.

To sum up, citizens in the Commonwealth of Massachusetts have a right to refuse treatment of any kind, even if their refusal will result in death. Psychiatric patients—even though committed to a hospital—have this right to the same degree as all other citizens. A psychiatric patient who is not competent will be given antipsychotic medication against his will in only two circumstances: to avoid "the immediate, substantial, and irreversible deterioration of a serious mental illness" or when a court has determined that the patient would take the medication if he were competent. The right to refuse treatment is alive and well in Massachusetts.

36. May restraints and seclusion be used for therapeutic purposes?

Section 21 of chapter 123 and 104 CMR 27.13 speak at considerable length about the use of restraints. 104 CMR 27.13 begins with a definition, "Restraint is a term that includes . . . four categories: mechanical restraint, physical restraint, seclusion and chemical restraint," while section 21 states that "restraint of a mentally ill person may *only* [italics added] be used in cases of emergency." Section 21 gives as examples of an emergency "the occurrence of, or serious threat of, extreme violence, personal injury, or attempted suicide." Restraints and seclusion may be used only to end or to prevent an emergency, and only then under the extensive restrictions laid out in section 21 of chapter 123 and 104 CMR 27.13. That restraints or seclusion are therapeutically indicated will *not* justify their use.

Mental health professionals should note, however, that by definition "restraint" is the unreasonable confinement of an individual's freedom to move. Restraint does not refer to orthopedically prescribed appliances necessary for treatment; supportive body bands; protective helmets; or physically holding when necessary for surgical purposes, medical treatment, and to achieve bodily position or proper balance to protect a patient from falling out of bed.

37. Chapter 123 gives a great deal of authority to mental health professionals. Could a patient who had been involuntarily sent to a hospital with a pink paper, involuntarily admitted to a psychiatric unit, or unwillingly placed in restraints, ever have cause to sue?

Section 22 of chapter 123 states, in its entirety:

Physicians, qualified psychologists and police officers shall be immune from civil suits for damages for restraining, transporting, applying for the admission of or admitting any person to a facility or the Bridgewater state hospital, providing said physician, qualified psychologist or police officer acts pursuant to the provisions of this chapter.

Chapter 123 thus insulates from liability psychiatrists, qualified psychologists, and police officers when, following the provisions of chapter 123, they engage in any of the stated activities. Clinicians authorized to sign pink papers and to admit patients under a section 12 must therefore take care to adhere to the requirements of chapter 123. *For this reason, becoming familiar with chapter 123 is well worth your time and effort if you intend to work with individuals who are likely to need psychiatric hospitalization.*

38. How should I handle a situation in which a client, who clearly meets commitment criteria, begins to get up and walk out of my office? Should I ever attempt physically to restrain a client?

The vast majority of mental health professionals are neither trained in the technique, nor legally authorized, to restrain a client. From a practical point of view, this lack of training increases the likelihood that someone will get injured if you attempt to restrain a client. From a legal point of view, you risk being sued for assault and battery should you attempt to restrain a client. *Do not attempt to do what you are neither trained nor authorized to do.*

If a client who appears to meet commitment criteria insists on leaving your office, call the people who are trained and authorized to use restraints: mental health workers at a community mental health center, security at a hospital, or the local police. Apprise the appropriate agency or services (e.g., the Boston Emergency Services Team) of the situation. As difficult as it is to watch such a client walk out of your office, best to use *your* expertise (in formulating a clinical assessment) to inform others so that they may use *their* expertise (in using restraints) to place your client in a safe setting.

Finally, recall that chapter 123, section 36B (see chapter 2) states explicitly that a mental health professional need not take any action that increases the likelihood that he will be harmed.

39. Does Massachusetts have a law providing for outpatient commitment?

There is no outpatient commitment in Massachusetts. *Outpatient commitment* requires an individual to comply with a treatment plan when *outside the walls* of a psychiatric unit. As an example, say that Phil (see question 32) was discharged from the hospital back to his group home under an outpatient commitment. Under his treatment plan, Phil is required to attend therapy sessions and to take his medication. If Phil stopped taking his medication, his doctor could contact the police who would then pick Phil up and bring him to the hospital. Once there, Phil would be given his medication, by force if necessary. With outpatient commitment, *noncompliance with a treatment plan is sufficient to initiate state intervention.*

The practical effect of not having outpatient commitment is that the Commonwealth will intervene only when an individual is believed to meet the criteria for civil commitment. Thus, in Massachusetts, an individual will be placed in a psychiatric hospital against her will only when she presents a risk to herself or to others. Moreover, an individual in Massachusetts will be forced to take medication only in an emergency or when a judge has determined that the patient, if competent, would choose to take her medication.

6

CRIMINAL LAW

Mental health professionals may be called upon to assess whether a criminal defendant is competent to stand trial or responsible for a crime he has committed. Competency to stand trial and criminal responsibility are often confused with one another. They are alike insofar as both require assessing a criminal defendant's state of mind. They differ insofar as competency to stand trial speaks to the defendant's state of mind <u>at the time of trial</u>, while criminal responsibility speaks to the defendant's state of mind <u>at the time of the crime</u>. An individual who is found not criminally responsible is referred to as "criminally insane," or simply "insane"; insanity is thus a <u>legal</u> concept with <u>legal</u> consequences.

M.G.L. chapter 123, section 15 says that a court may order an examination to determine whether a defendant is competent to stand trial or criminally insane.

QUESTIONS DISCUSSED IN THIS CHAPTER

40. What is the Massachusetts test for insanity?
41. What happens to a person who is found criminally insane?
42. When is a person not competent to stand trial?

43. **What happens to a person who is found not competent to stand trial?**
44. **What happens if someone in a jail or prison becomes depressed, has a psychotic break, or otherwise needs mental health services?**

DISCUSSION

40. What is the Massachusetts test for insanity?

When do we say that an individual is not blameworthy for what he did? If a person becomes psychotic and assaults a complete stranger, is he criminally insane? If a person steals a car while in a manic state, should she be sent to jail? If a person commits a murder while dissociating, and later remembers nothing, is prison an appropriate response?

The most well-known Massachusetts case on the insanity defense is *Commonwealth v. McHoul*, 352 Mass. 544 (1967), from which derives what has come to be known as the "McHoul test." In *McHoul*, the SJC adopted the following standard for insanity:

> "(1) A person is not responsible for criminal conduct if at the time of such conduct as a result of mental disease or defect he lacks substantial capacity either to appreciate the criminality [wrongfulness] of his conduct or to conform his conduct to the requirements of the law." (*McHoul* at 546–547, quoting section 401 of the American Law Institute's Model Penal Code)

There are four things to note about the McHoul test. First, the nonresponsibility must arise from a "mental disease or defect." If the individual does not suffer from a mental disease or defect, then he cannot be found insane. Second, in virtue of the mental disease or defect, the individual must lack "substantial capacity . . . to appreciate . . . or to conform." It is not enough to show that the mental disease or defect merely *affects* an individual's capacities along these dimensions; the effect must be *substantial*. Third, the test has both cognitive ("to appreciate") and behavioral ("to conform") components. Fourth, the lack in capacity may be *either* cognitive (the capacity to appreciate) *or* behavioral (the capacity to conform)— it need not be both. A substantial deficit in either capacity brought about by mental disease or defect is enough to warrant a finding of criminal nonresponsibility.

41. What happens to a person who is found criminally insane?

The answer to this question has generated an enormous amount of debate in recent years. The fuel behind the fire is a belief that too many people are found not criminally responsible, that is, are judged criminally insane, and therefore go free. This belief is not supported by the facts. About one percent of criminal defendants plead insanity, and the plea is successful in only 25% of those cases. Thus, the insanity plea is relevant to only one quarter of one percent of criminal defendants. Moreover, as the answer to the question will indicate, defendants are not free to walk after a finding of insanity. Far from it. Criminal defendants found insane are most often placed in maximum security treatment facilities.

M.G.L. chapter 123, section 16 provides that following an acquittal by reason of mental illness the (former) criminal defendant may be hospitalized for 40 days "for observation and examination." Within 60 days of the acquittal the district attorney (the lawyer who prosecuted the case) or the superintendent of the hospital where the person has been sent for observation and examination may ask that the individual be committed. This commitment, the standards for which are the same as for civil commitment (see question 23), is for up to six months; subsequent commitments are for up to one year. The kicker—again something not commonly known by the public—is that an individual acquitted by reason of mental illness may be held for a longer period of time in a mental hospital than he would have served had he been found guilty and sent to jail or prison.

42. When is a person not competent to stand trial?

To be competent to stand trial in Massachusetts, a person must be able to assume the role of a criminal defendant. Assuming this role requires the capacity to understand the nature of the judicial proceedings and to assist one's attorney—if a person is able neither to understand what's going on around him, nor to help his attorney put on a defense, the trial isn't a fair trial. In *Commonwealth v. Vailes*, 360 Mass. 522 (1971), the SJC adopted this two-part test from a United States Supreme Court case called *Dusky v. United States*, 362 U.S. 402 (1960). In *Dusky*, the U.S. Supreme Court held that, in determining whether a criminal defendant is competent to stand trial, a court should ask:

> whether [the defendant] has sufficient present ability to consult with his lawyer with a reasonable degree of rational understanding and

whether he has a rational as well as factual understanding of the proceedings against him. (402)

Examples of questions that would help to assess competence to stand trial would therefore be: Is the defendant able to understand that the prosecutor thinks he has done something wrong? Is the defendant able to understand that his attorney is there to help him? Is the defendant able to understand that he may be put in jail, or told to pay a fine, if he is found guilty? Is the defendant able to sit in court and listen to what other people say about him, or to what people claim he did? Is the defendant able to answer questions his attorney may need to ask him in order to put on a defense?

Notice how the first three questions begin with, "Is the defendant able to understand . . . ," rather than, "Does the defendant know that . . ." The reason for beginning the questions in this manner is that competency to stand trial is based on what the individual is *able* to understand about the judicial process, not on what he *actually* understands. If a person does not actually understand something about the trial, but can come to understand this information, you may educate him. *Competence is a capacity.*

43. What happens to a person who is found not competent to stand trial?

M.G.L. chapter 123, section 16 says that if an individual is found not competent to stand trial, the court may order that he be hospitalized for up to 40 days "for observation and examination." According to section 16, within 60 days after a court finds the individual incompetent to stand trial, the district attorney or the superintendent of the hospital may ask that the individual be committed. The court may order that the individual stay in a jail or hospital while the commitment process moves forward. The court will then decide about commitment in the same way it decides about the commitment of any other individual. The initial commitment is for up to six months; subsequent commitments are for periods of up to one year. If the individual becomes competent to stand trial, he goes back to court and the criminal proceedings resume. Thus, like individuals found criminally insane, individuals found incompetent to stand trial are not simply released. A number of provisions allow for their continued confinement either in jail or in a hospital.

One caveat: Section 16 states that the court case against the individual found incompetent to stand trial must be dismissed (thrown out) no later than the time the person would have been eligible for parole had he "been

---

COMPETENCE TO STAND TRIAL AND CRIMINAL RESPONSIBILITY

I. Involve **criminal** proceedings (person has been charged with a crime).

II. Involve assessment of person's mental state at a given point in time:
   A. **At time of conduct alleged to be a crime** (criminal responsibility).
   B. **At time of trial** (competence to stand trial).

III. Involve assessment of mental capacity.
   A. Person not criminally responsible (insane) if:
      1. Suffers from a **mental disease or defect;**
      2. As a result of mental disease or defect, person lacks **substantial** capacity:
         i. To **appreciate** the wrongfulness of his conduct; *or*
         ii. To **conform his conduct** to the requirements of the law.
   B. Person not competent to stand trial if:
      1. Does not have sufficient present ability to **consult with his lawyer** with a reasonable degree of rational understanding and;
      2. Does not have a rational as well as factual **understanding of the proceedings** against him.

---

convicted of the most serious crime with which he was charged . . . and sentenced to the maximum sentence he would have received," combined with certain statutory provisions that reduce the length of imprisonment (e.g., for good behavior). This limitation found in section 16 prevents an individual from being confined permanently to a hospital in the hopes that he will someday become competent to stand trial. If the person is to be kept in the hospital longer than he would have been in jail had he been found guilty, there must be grounds for hospitalization independent of his incompetence to stand trial.

44. What happens if someone in a jail or prison becomes depressed, has a psychotic break, or otherwise needs mental health services?

No Massachusetts law requires that mental health services be provided in jails or prisons. Section 18 of chapter 123 provides that if an inmate is "in need of hospitalization by reason of mental illness," the person in charge of the jail or prison can arrange to have the inmate examined by a psychologist or a psychiatrist. The ensuing report is sent to a court, which can order that the inmate be transferred from the jail to a hospital and examined for up to 30 days, either at Bridgewater or some other state hospital if further evaluation is indicated. In addition, section 18 provides that any inmate who needs care may apply for voluntary admission to a hospital if the person in charge of the jail or prison grants permission.

An inmate who is hospitalized may only be kept involuntarily for the length of his sentence, minus time for certain sentence reductions (e.g., for good behavior). He must then be released unless he meets commitment criteria. If, before his sentence has expired, the inmate no longer needs treatment, he is returned whence he came, to jail.

7

SUBPOENAS AND COURT ORDERS

As you read these questions, recall (from chapter 3) the close relationship between confidentiality and testimonial privilege. To say that a communication is "confidential" means that the mental health professional cannot disclose the communication without the client's consent. To say that a communication is "protected by testimonial privilege" means that the mental health professional cannot disclose the communication in a legal proceeding without the client's consent. When a client allows a mental health professional to disclose communications that are protected by privilege, the client is said to "waive privilege." If a client "invokes privilege," the mental health professional may not reveal the communication.

QUESTIONS DISCUSSED IN THIS CHAPTER

51. **What if a patient decides to waive privilege for only *part* of the record?**
52. **Is a court order different from a subpoena?**
53. **Is a court order like a subpoena insofar as either the entire record, or none of the record at all, will be released?**

DISCUSSION

45. What is a subpoena?

The word "subpoena" comes from the two Latin words "sub" and "poena" which, taken together, mean "under a penalty." A subpoena is a legal process granted to lawyers in order to conduct discovery (see question 7) or to have a witness appear at trial. An individual who does not comply with a subpoena may be placed under a penalty, which may be a fine, arrest, and even jail. A special kind of subpoena, a subpoena *duces tecum*, requires that an individual bring certain materials with him either to a deposition or to a trial. Important to note is that a subpoena is a requirement: that you appear at a given place at a given time (subpoena); or that you appear at such place and time with specified materials (subpoena duces tecum).

A sample subpoena is included in appendix B.

46. If I receive a subpoena should I go ahead and do whatever it says?

No—you need to worry about your client's confidentiality! A subpoena is a demand for your *appearance*; once you have *appeared* you have complied with the subpoena. Although a subpoena is a very scary looking piece of paper, it *neither requires nor allows you to reply to questions or to produce materials that are protected by testimonial privilege*. You may only answer questions or produce materials if your client grants you permission (waives privilege) or a court orders you to do so. If your client decides to waive privilege, you will ask him to do so in writing (see question 50).

Lawyers who do not understand or who choose to ignore the concept of testimonial privilege may insist (rant and rave, jump up and down, threaten you with contempt) that you provide the information they want. Simply explain that you are not able to do so without your client's consent or a court order, and ask the lawyer to contact your—or your client's—attorney with any further questions.

47. What's the first thing to do if I receive a subpoena?

Inform your client that you have received the subpoena and indicate what the subpoena demands. Next, determine if your records and testimony are protected by testimonial privilege (see chapter 3). If your client is willing to waive privilege, that is, to allow you to disclose information protected by testimonial privilege, you may then go ahead and do what the subpoena asks. Make sure your client waives privilege in writing (see question 50). If your client invokes privilege—does *not* allow you to testify or release records—have your client's lawyer contact you and proceed as directed. If your client does not have a lawyer, contact your own lawyer. *Under no circumstances should you contact the lawyer who issued the subpoena, except in writing and only then for the purpose of stating that, unless you receive the patient's permission or an order from the court, you will not release or disclose any information protected by testimonial privilege. You may also request to be released from the subpoena (see question 49).*

48. What if I cannot locate my client?

Remember that *privilege belongs to the client.* You therefore cannot waive privilege for your client—only your client may give you permission to testify or to release records. If you cannot find your client (perhaps because the treatment has terminated and your client has moved), you may invoke privilege on your client's behalf. In this case you do not testify or release records until a court orders you to do so.

49. Once my client has invoked privilege, or I have invoked privilege on my client's behalf, do I need to do anything else?

Even though your client has invoked privilege, or you have invoked privilege on your client's behalf, the subpoena remains valid insofar as a subpoena's demand is for your *appearance.* Once privilege is invoked, you may contact the attorney who issued the subpoena and request that you be "released" from the subpoena. If you are able, get the release in writing; if you are not able to get the release in writing, make a note of the day and the time of the release in your records. Most lawyers will not force you to appear at a deposition or trial until it has been determined what materials will be disclosed.

50. What do I actually do to comply with a subpoena?

When your client says that he intends to waive privilege, tell him that you would like a letter to that effect, and that you will provide him a copy of the subpoena to review and attach to his letter. The letter need not be long—essential ingredients are: the date, your client's signature, and a statement that he waives privilege and thereby allows you to comply with the attached subpoena. It is important to remember that unless your client is under guardianship, only he can waive privilege, so that only *his* signature on the letter will suffice.

51. What if a patient decides to waive privilege for only *part* of the record?

Privilege cannot be waived in part. This point is important and separates privilege from confidentiality. A patient may ask that a treater only discuss certain confidential information with, for example, an employer or a family member. Testimonial privilege is different. A patient either waives privilege or she does not. If a patient voluntarily testifies to a privileged matter, then the matter is opened to a full inquiry, testimonial privilege notwithstanding. For this reason, patients must be extremely careful when they speak in any sort of legal proceeding. Once the floodgates have opened, it may be impossible to close them.

52. Is a court order different from a subpoena?

Yes—while an *attorney* issues a subpoena, a *judge* issues a court order after a proceeding called a "fair hearing." At a fair hearing a judge decides if the communication under review is protected by testimonial privilege. To make this determination, the judge may ask: Is the mental health professional licensed? Did the communication take place in the context of a professional relationship? Does the mental health professional belong to a discipline named by one of the privilege statutes? If the answer to any of these questions is "no," the judge may decide that the communication is *not* protected by privilege, which means that it may be introduced into the legal proceeding. If the judge determines that the communication *is* protected by privilege, she will then determine whether any exception to privilege applies. An exception to privilege would permit the communication to be introduced.

If the judge determines that the communication is not privileged, or that the communication, while privileged, falls under an exception, she will order the record, or part of the record, to be produced. If the judge determines that the communication *is* protected by testimonial privilege, and that no exception applies, she will "quash" (think "squash") the subpoena, and you need not do anything else.

Bottom line: The judge will either order you to produce all or part of the record or she will quash the subpoena. Her word is final, and you do what she says.

53. Is a court order like a subpoena insofar as either the entire record, or none of the record at all, will be released?

No, and this difference is extremely important. A court order will specify what material from the record is to be released. *You only release material specified in the court order.* Whenever you receive an order from a court, you must read the order carefully and follow its instructions exactly.

8

GUARDIANS, CONSERVATORS, AND SUBSTITUTE DECISION-MAKING

*One of the fundamental values upon which our society is built is
<u>individual autonomy</u>. Individuals are allowed great leeway in the
choices they may make: how to worship, what to read, where to live,
whom to marry. In our society these and many, many other choices
belong to the individual. Because of the value we place on individual
autonomy, we presume that individuals are competent to make the
choices necessary for living their lives in whatever fashion they choose.*

*The presumption of competence holds until we have evidence to the
contrary. When such evidence comes to light, and we have reason to
believe that an individual is not competent to make important decisions, the state looks to its <u>parens patriae</u> power, its authority to take
care of individuals who are not capable of caring for themselves.
Under the <u>parens patriae</u> power the state may appoint a substitute
decision-maker, such as a guardian or a conservator. Also, through
such instruments as a health care proxy and a durable power of
attorney, the law allows an individual to anticipate and plan for his
own incapacity to make decisions.*

QUESTIONS DISCUSSED IN THIS CHAPTER

54. Where are the laws that govern guardians and conservators?
55. May a guardian be appointed for anyone?
56. Who may serve as a guardian?
57. Which court has jurisdiction over appointing guardians for mentally ill persons?
58. Who may ask that a guardian be appointed for a mentally ill person?
59. How does the probate court decide whether to appoint a guardian for a mentally ill person?
60. What standard of proof must be met before a court will decide that a guardianship is warranted or a mentally ill person?
61. What is a temporary guardian?
62. How long does a guardianship last?
63. What decisions does a guardian make?
64. What medical treatment may a guardian authorize for a mentally ill person?
65. How does a treater know when a patient needs a Rogers order?
66. How does a treater obtain a Rogers order?
67. What is the difference between a Rogers order obtained under c.201, §6 and a Rogers order obtained under c.123, §8B?
68. How does a probate court or a district court decide whether to approve a treater's request for a Rogers order?
69. How closely should a treater work with a guardian?
70. If a patient under guardianship does not follow the treatment plan calling for antipsychotic medication, what can the guardian do?
71. If a patient agrees to treatment with antipsychotic medication, is a Rogers necessary?
72. Does a guardian have the authority to commit a mentally ill individual to a psychiatric hospital?
73. When can a guardian commit her ward to a psychiatric hospital?
74. Does every patient who is committed to a psychiatric hospital need a guardian and a Rogers order?
75. What's the difference between an inpatient guardianship and an outpatient guardianship?
76. What is a guardian ad litem?
77. What is a conservator?
78. What is a representative payee?
79. What is a health care proxy?
80. When does a health care proxy end?
81. What is a durable power of attorney?

DISCUSSION

54. Where are the laws that govern guardians and conservators?

The laws governing guardians and conservators are found in chapter 201 of the Massachusetts General Laws, titled, fittingly enough, "Guardians and Conservators." Chapter 201 discusses the various types of guardians and conservators, as well as the rules that govern how guardians and conservators get appointed and do their work. Also relevant to the topic of guardians and conservators is case law. The most well-known case in this area is *Rogers v. Commissioner of the Department of Mental Health*, 390 Mass. 489 (1983). The significance of the Rogers case will be explained in greater detail below.

55. May a guardian be appointed for anyone?

Chapter 201, section 1 lists five groups of people for whom a guardian may be appointed. These groups are: "minors, mentally ill persons, mentally retarded persons, persons unable to make or communicate informed decisions due to physical incapacity or illness, and spendthrifts." Section 8 of chapter 201 defines a spendthrift as an individual who "by excessive drinking, gaming, idleness, or debauchery of any kind, so spends, wastes or lessens his estate as to expose himself or his family to want or suffering."

The person on behalf of whom the guardian has been appointed is referred to as the "ward."

56. Who may serve as a guardian?

Any individual whom the probate court deems "suitable" may serve as a guardian. An individual is frequently deemed suitable because no reason speaks *against* that individual's appointment: The individual is competent, has no conflict with the ward, is able to get along reasonably well with significant persons in the ward's life, and so forth.

Many guardians are lawyers, although many are mental health professionals. Family members often serve as guardians. The value of appointing a family member (or close friend) as a guardian is that these individuals may have a good sense of the ward's wants, needs, and desires. Familiarity with a ward's preferences is especially useful when the treatment plan involves administering antipsychotic medication. Mental health professionals, particularly social workers, are often appointed as guardians in other special situations, such as those that involve child visitation.

57. Which court has jurisdiction over appointing guardians for mentally ill persons?

Chapter 201, section 6 gives the probate court jurisdiction over appointing guardians for mentally ill persons.

58. Who may ask that a guardian be appointed for a mentally ill person?

Chapter 201, section 6 states that any of the following may ask a probate court to appoint a guardian for a mentally ill person: a parent; two or more friends; two or more relatives; a nonprofit organization whose corporate charter allows it to act as a guardian; and any state agency within the executive office of human services or educational affairs.

59. How does the probate court decide whether to appoint a guardian for a mentally ill person?

Chapter 201, section 6 sets forth the test by which the probate court determines whether a guardian should be appointed for a mentally ill person. Perhaps the most important provision of the test found in section 6 is that mental illness alone will not warrant a guardianship. The individual must be *both* mentally ill *and* "incapable of taking care of himself by reason of mental illness." A careful reading of section 6 thus shows that three elements must be present before a guardian may be appointed: First, the individual must be *mentally ill*; second, the individual must be *incapable of taking care of himself*; and third, there must be a *causal connection* between the individual's mental illness and his inability to take care of himself. In Fazio v. Fazio 375 Mass. 394 (1978), the SJC interpreted the language of section 6:

> [T]he type of evidence necessary to support [appointing a guardian], apart from evidence as to mental illness, should consist of facts showing a proposed ward's inability to think or act for himself as to matters concerning his personal health, safety, and general welfare, or to make informed decisions as to his property or financial interests. (403; footnote omitted)

When a guardian is appointed to make decisions only about the ward's personal health, safety, and welfare, it is said that the guardianship "is limited to the person only." Otherwise, the guardianship is of "the person and the estate," also referred to as a "full guardianship."

60. What standard of proof must be met before a court will decide that a guardianship is warranted for a mentally ill person?

In *Guardianship of Roe*, 383 Mass. 415 (1981), the SJC held that the standard of proof in a guardianship hearing is a preponderance of the evidence, also referred to as "more likely than not" (see question 4). A preponderance of evidence is the lowest standard of proof in our legal system, and requires that a mere 51% of the evidence weigh in on the side of the party asking that a guardian be appointed. The standard of proof selected by the SJC reflects its values—when in doubt, the SJC would rather err on the side of appointing a guardian. The SJC's reasoning is straightforward: Individuals who should have a guardian appointed, but do not, will suffer more harm than individuals who should *not* have a guardian appointed, but do.

61. What is a temporary guardian?

A permanent guardianship often takes several months to obtain. The reason is that appointing a guardian is a serious matter, and numerous procedural requirements must be met along the way. When a guardian must be appointed immediately, the probate court may appoint a *temporary guardian* under section 14 of chapter 201. A temporary guardianship is focused and limited, insofar as its purpose is to address a specific harm. According to section 14:

> Whenever a temporary guardian is so appointed, [the probate court's] decree or order shall indicate the nature of the emergency requiring such appointment and the particular harm sought be avoided, and shall state that the temporary guardian so appointed is only authorized to take such actions with regard to the ward as are reasonably necessary to avoid the occurrence of that harm.

Often the purpose of a temporary guardianship is to serve as a "bridge" until a permanent guardian can be appointed.

62. How long does a guardianship last?

A *permanent guardianship* will last for as long as the ward remains incompetent, and so in need of a guardian. When it appears that a ward has returned to competence, section 13 of chapter 201 allows the probate court to hold a hearing. If, at the hearing, the probate court finds that the ward has returned to competence, it will revoke the guardianship. A *temporary guardianship* is valid for 90 days and may be extended for one additional 90-day period. A temporary guardianship would also end were a permanent guardian to be appointed.

63. What decisions does a guardian make?

A guardian will make decisions "as to matters concerning [the ward's] personal health, safety, and welfare and . . . as to his property or financial interests" (*Fazio*, at 403). Decisions regarding the ward's "personal health, safety, and welfare," may involve determining where a ward will live, what type of treatment a ward will receive for routine medical conditions, and where a ward will travel. A guardian will *not* make decisions concerning matters that do not affect the ward's personal health, safety, or welfare, such as what clothes a ward wears, what posters a ward puts up on his bedroom walls, or whom a ward has dinner with.

A guardian will also make decisions "as to [the ward's] property or financial interests." These decisions may involve when to sell a piece of the ward's property, when to spend the ward's money for upkeep on the ward's house or apartment, or when to enter into a contract for professional services on the ward's behalf.

64. What medical treatment may a guardian authorize for a mentally ill person?

A guardian may authorize usual and customary, or routine, medical treatment. Such treatment would include routine diagnostic tests, minor surgery, or admittance to a general hospital or nursing home when medically indicated. A guardian may *not* authorize "extraordinary" medical treatment. The SJC has defined a number of treatments as "extraordinary"; generally, any treatment that entails a risk of significant pain, significant harm, or likelihood that a permanent change in the ward's mental or physical functioning will result is considered "extraordinary." In *Rogers v. Commissioner of the Department of Mental Health* 390 Mass. 489 (1983), the SJC held that treatment with antipsychotic medication is "extraordinary," and so *cannot* be authorized by a guardian. *Only a court can authorize extraordinary treatment for an individual who is incompetent; hence, only a court can authorize treatment with antipsychotic medication for a mentally ill person under guardianship.* A "Rogers" order—so named for the court case—refers to a court order authorizing treatment with antipsychotic medication.

Electroshock therapy and psychosurgery are also considered "extraordinary" medical treatments.

65. How does a treater know when a patient needs a Rogers order?

Every competent adult has the right to decide on his medical treatment. As part of that right, every person is entitled to informed consent concerning the type, nature, and degree of treatment. Thus, treatment with antipsychotic medication requires the treater to obtain informed consent. Informed consent entails knowing the nature and purpose of a proposed treatment, the risks and benefits of that treatment, the risks and benefits of alternate treatments, and the risks and benefits of no treatment at all. Note that obtaining informed consent does not require that the patient quote from the *PDR* or the *DSM-IV*; take as an example a patient prescribed Clozaril for auditory hallucinations. Asked to explain this treatment, the patient replied:

> These pills are to help make the voices I sometimes hear when nobody's around go away. Every week I have to go and have my blood taken because this medicine can make me get sick and the doctors need to know what my blood cell count is to keep me healthy. I used to take other medication, but it made me shake, and I would worry about getting "TD," a disease where your mouth and face move a lot, and you can't stop them. If I didn't take any medication at all, the voices would be real bad, and I could hardly think or do anything.

Note how this patient's response contains all the elements of an informed decision to accept the Clozaril.

When a person's illness appears to compromise that individual's ability to understand important treatment information or to communicate desires about the treatment, the clinician must decide whether the individual is able to comprehend the information and give consent. If you determine that an individual is not able to give consent, you must consider seeking a Rogers order.

66. How does a treater obtain a Rogers order?

A treater may obtain a Rogers order either through section 6 of chapter 201 or through section 8B of chapter 123. These two paths have four characteristics in common. First, the clinician will put forth in writing the reasons why she believes that the individual is not competent to make treatment decisions. Second, the clinician will set forth, again in writing, the proposed treatment plan with as much specificity as possible about what antipsychotic medications are to be used. Third, the court—not the guardian or the treaters—authorizes the actual treatment with antipsychotic medication. Fourth, the role of the guardian is to *monitor* the treatment plan—not to administer the medication. Because of their role monitoring medication, guardians appointed under a Rogers order are sometimes referred to as "med" guardians.

67. What is the difference between a Rogers order obtained under c.201, §6 and a Rogers order obtained under c.123, §8B?

There are three important differences. First, a Rogers order issued under chapter 201, section 6 is issued as part of a general guardianship proceeding. A Rogers order issued through chapter 123, section 8B is issued when the individual is on an inpatient psychiatric unit, and may only be issued in conjunction with a commitment order by the court. Second, the probate court, which has jurisdiction over guardianship proceedings, issues a Rogers order obtained under section 6. The district court, which has jurisdiction over civil commitment proceedings, issues a Rogers order under section 8B. Third, a Rogers order issued under section 6 will expire when indicated by the treatment plan approved by the probate court. Treatment plans authorized under section 6 as part of a guardianship proceeding must be reviewed by the court at least once each year. As a consequence, if the treatment plan approved by the probate court does not have an expiration date, the yearly court review will either extend or terminate the Rogers order. A Rogers order under section 8B will expire when the order for civil commitment expires, in either six months or one year, or when the individual is discharged from the hospital, whichever occurs first.

68. How does a probate court or a district court decide whether to approve a treater's request for a Rogers order?

Traditionally, guardians have made decisions in one of two ways: either according to what is best for their ward or according to what their ward would have chosen, if competent. The former way of making decisions is referred to as the "best interests" standard, while the latter way of making decisions is referred to as the "substituted judgment" standard. In *Rogers*, the SJC came down decidedly in favor of the substituted judgment standard. In deciding whether to approve treatment with antipsychotic medication, courts must attempt to determine *what the individual would choose if he were competent.* In *Rogers,* the SJC identified six factors as important for courts to consider in making their substituted judgment determinations: (1) the patient's expressed preferences regarding treatment, (2) the patient's religious convictions, (3) the impact of the decision on the patient's family, (4) the probability of adverse side effects, (5) the prognosis without treatment, and (6) the prognosis with treatment. The SJC also said that the court could consider "any other factors which appear relevant" (*Rogers* at 505–506).

69. How closely should a treater work with a guardian?

In Massachusetts, decisions that involve extraordinary treatment are made on the substituted judgment standard—that is to say, decisions about extraordinary treatment (e.g., antipsychotic medication) are based upon *what the ward would decide, if he were competent.* Other decisions (e.g., where the ward will live) are usually made on the best interests standard. In either case, treaters should work closely with the guardian: in the former, because the guardian is substituting for the ward himself; in the latter, because the guardian needs to have the information necessary to determine what will be in the ward's best interests.

70. If a patient under guardianship does not follow the treatment plan calling for antipsychotic medication, what can the guardian do?

Under both chapter 201, section 6 and chapter 123, section 8B, the role of the guardian is to *monitor* the treatment plan. Thus, the guardian will never be in the position of administering antipsychotic medication to the ward, or of punishing the ward for not taking the medication. The guardian may, however, inform the court of the ward's noncompliance with the treatment plan.

That said, what happens in practice usually depends upon whether the Rogers order is obtained through chapter 201, section 6 or chapter 123, section 8B. If the Rogers is through section 8B, the setting is an inpatient unit. In this case the clinicians may forcibly medicate by whatever reasonable means necessary, including holding the patient and injecting the medication. If the Rogers is through section 6 and the patient is already in the hospital, the patient may be treated under the same authority as if he were under an 8B. If the patient is not in the hospital, the guardian may attempt to persuade the ward to take the medication or go to the hospital.

71. If a patient agrees to treatment with antipsychotic medication, is a Rogers necessary?

Be sure to distinguish between "assent" and "consent." A patient may *assent*—agree—to treatment with antipsychotic medication without having the slightest idea why in the world you keep giving him those little blue pills three times a day. *Consent* implies that the patient understands a good deal about the treatment—its nature and purpose, its risks and benefits, and so forth (see question 65). *Assent* does not necessarily entail *consent.*

Every patient is entitled to informed consent. If a patient cannot give informed consent—*assent* notwithstanding—a Rogers order is necessary. Don't be fooled—that a patient agrees to take what you give is not dispositive on the important issue, namely, whether the patient is capable of giving informed consent.

72. Does a guardian have the authority to commit a mentally ill individual to a psychiatric hospital?

Section 6 of chapter 201 allows the probate court to authorize a guardian to "admit or commit" a ward to a psychiatric hospital. A guardian only has the authority to "admit or commit," however, when specifically authorized by the probate court—the authority to "admit or commit" does not come automatically with the appointment of a guardian.

73. When can a guardian commit her ward to a psychiatric hospital?

A guardian can commit her ward to a psychiatric hospital when specifically authorized to do so by the probate court. The guardian must demonstrate that the ward meets the commitment criteria set forth in chapter 123, namely, that failure to hospitalize would create a likelihood of serious harm.

A guardian may not commit a ward to a psychiatric hospital because the guardian likes the idea, thinks it would be in the ward's best interests, or believes that the ward needs treatment. Rather, the guardian can only do so when the probate court has determined that the ward meets commitment criteria and has explicitly given the guardian this authority.

74. Does every patient who is committed to a psychiatric hospital need a guardian and a Rogers order?

Admission or commitment to a psychiatric hospital does not necessarily warrant the appointment of a guardian. Section 24 of chapter 123 makes this point clearly: "No person shall be deemed incompetent to manage his affairs . . . solely by reason of his admission or commitment . . . to any public or private facility." A person remains competent to manage his affairs until a judge decides otherwise.

Nor does commitment to a psychiatric hospital, in and of itself, necessitate a Rogers order. The reason is that the standard for civil commitment (risk to self or others), and the standard for a Rogers order (inability to give informed consent) are *different* standards. Chapter 123, sections 8B and 24 make clear that an individual committed to a psychiatric hospital *may be perfectly competent* to make decisions about treatment with antipsychotic medication. Put another way, one may both present a risk to self or others and be able to give informed consent. Incompetence to make treatment decisions—not risk of harm—is the touchstone for determining whether to obtain a Rogers order.

Note also the converse—just because a guardian is appointed, or a Rogers order issued, does not mean that the individual must be committed to a psychiatric hospital. Again, three different standards govern.

STANDARDS FOR STATE INTERVENTION

I. Civil committment: Failure to hospitalize/discharge from hospital creates liklihood of serious harm (c.123 §§7 and 8). (*Risk of harm to self or others by reason of mental illness*)

II. Guardianship: Individual not able either:
   a. to think or act for self as to matters concerning personal health, safety, and general welfare <u>or</u>
   b. to make informed decision as to his property or financial interests.

III. Rogers order: Individual not able to give informed consent about treatment with antipsychotic medication.

---

75. What's the difference between an inpatient guardianship and an outpatient guardianship?

An inpatient guardianship refers to a guardian who has the authority to "admit or commit" the ward to a psychiatric hospital (see question 72). Note that not all guardians have this authority. Certain guardians, for example, are appointed to monitor the ward's antipsychotic medication, or to make decisions about where the ward will live, roles that may not involve hospitalization. An outpatient guardianship thus refers to a guardian who—whatever responsibilities she may have—does not have the authority to "admit or commit."

76. What is a guardian ad litem?

A guardian ad litem is a special type of guardian appointed by the probate court. The words "ad litem" are Latin and refer to a legal proceeding. A guardian ad litem ensures that a ward's legal rights are represented during a matter before the probate court.

A guardian ad litem (GAL) is usually (but not always) a lawyer. Unlike other guardians, a GAL does not treat or act on the ward's behalf. Rather, a GAL is the *court's* investigator; the probate court hires a GAL to gather information and make recommendations. For this reason, GALs are sometimes referred to as the "eyes and ears of the court." By having a GAL review the record, interview the ward, speak with individuals involved in the ward's care, and perhaps travel to the ward's residence, the court can be sure that all aspects of a case will come to light and that a ward's rights will thereby be protected.

GALs are usually empowered to review a patient's records and to discuss treatment issues with the clinicians. Mental health professionals should be sure to request a copy of the GAL appointment, however, before engaging in conversation or releasing records.

77. What is a conservator?

The probate court appoints a conservator for an individual who is "unable to properly care for his property" because of either "mental weakness" or "physical incapacity." The purpose of a conservator is to make property or financial decisions for the ward. Note that, unlike a guardian, a conservator will not make decisions concerning the "person" of the ward, that is, where the ward will live, what medical treatment the ward will receive, and the like.

Conservators differ from guardians in another important respect. According to section 16 of chapter 201, individuals who are unable to care for their property may *voluntarily* agree to have a conservator appointed. This provision is important, insofar as it distinguishes individuals who need a guardian because of incompetence from persons who, while remaining competent, need help with important business or financial decisions. A competent individual may thus have a conservator. In addition to the possibility of a competent individual voluntarily agreeing to the appointment of a conservator, the probate court may also appoint a conservator without the ward's consent if the ward suffers from "mental weakness."

78. What is a representative payee?

A representative payee (or "rep. payee") is a person or an agency who accepts payment from entitlement programs on behalf of a ward. An individual need not have a guardian, or be incompetent, to have a rep. payee; rather, the standard is whether having a rep. payee is judged in the person's interests. According to the Social Security Act, a rep. payee is automatically judged to be in the interests of an individual whose disability consists of drug or alcohol addiction.

79. What is a health care proxy?

A health care proxy is a document by which one person gives to another person the authority to make health care decisions. A health care proxy comes into play when the person handing over the authority becomes unable to make or to communicate decisions about medical treatment. The person who authors the health care proxy is called the "principal"; the person designated to make health care decisions in the event of the principal's incapacity is called the "agent." The guidelines for health care proxies are set forth in M.G.L. c.201D.

The value of a health care proxy is that it allows an individual to choose a trusted friend or relative to make medical decisions when the individual herself cannot. The individual writing the health care proxy can place any limitations she chooses on the agent's authority. Only a doctor—not the agent—may decide that the individual is incapable of making health care decisions, and the doctor must do so in writing. Only at that point does the health care proxy become effective.

80. When does a health care proxy end?

A health care proxy may be revoked at any time, *including after the principal has been deemed incompetent*. Any action by the principal indicating revocation is sufficient to cancel a health care proxy. The principal need only state to the agent or health care provider that the health care proxy is no longer in effect, tear the health care proxy up, throw the health care proxy away, or do anything else that indicates revocation. A health care proxy will also end if an individual writes another health care proxy, or if the agent and the principal are married, and the two get divorced.

81. What is a durable power of attorney?

A power of attorney is a document by which a principal authorizes an agent to perform acts having to do with the principal's property. Examples include writing checks and selling property. A power of attorney cannot be used to make health care decisions. The principal is bound by what the agent does, in the same way the principal would be bound if she herself had performed the acts. The power of attorney will specify precisely what the agent is allowed to do on behalf of the principal.

A *durable* power of attorney is a power of attorney that continues to be valid when the principal becomes disabled, for example by mental illness or dementia. A durable power of attorney may commence *upon* the principal's disability, or may remain valid *despite* the principal's disability. Whichever the case, the agent is authorized to act on the principal's behalf during a period of the principal's disability. As with a power of attorney, the principal is bound by what the agent does, in the same way as the principal would be bound if she herself had performed the acts.

Chapter 201B of the Massachusetts General Laws is the "Uniform Durable Power of Attorney Act."

9

CONSULTATION AND SUPERVISION

From a risk management perspective, the value of a consultation cannot be overemphasized. Every mental health professional has a legal duty to provide care that is reasonable. If a mental health professional's care falls below that which is reasonable, she may then be held responsible for any damages that result from her negligence. How do we determine whether a clinician's care is "reasonable"? By looking to the professional community. The standard set by the community of mental health professionals will determine what care is reasonable, and any individual clinician's care will be judged against that standard. Consultations are so valuable because they provide a link between an individual clinician and the community. In other words, <u>consultations bring a clinician into the professional fold</u>.

Consultations are particularly helpful in difficult treatments or when there is a transference or countertransference problem. Consultations show that the treater was working in a thoughtful manner, that she made an effort to reach out to her professional community, and that she was aware enough to know that a difficult aspect of the treatment— perhaps a countertransference issue—needed to be looked at from a perspective other than her own. A consultation is also powerful evi-

dence against a claim that a mental health professional was exploiting a patient or using the transference for personal gain. Exploitation is usually shrouded in secret; consultations provide a way of bringing a treatment into the open, thus serving to refute a suggestion or innuendo that the mental health professional was behaving unethically. Supervision, which places an entire treatment under the scrutiny of another mental health professional, plays much the same role as a consultation from the perspective of risk management.

QUESTIONS DISCUSSED IN THIS CHAPTER

82. **What rules of confidentiality govern consultations?**
83. **From a professional liability perspective, what is the difference between a consultation and supervision?**
84. **Is a trainee required to tell a patient that the treatment is being supervised?**
85. **What is negligent supervision? What would be an example of negligent supervision?**
86. **Treaters often keep notes of their own countertransference fantasies, separate from the record. These are neither progress nor process notes; their purpose is to help the treater gauge the nature and intensity of her own psychic processes as they relate to the clinical work. Could a lawyer ever obtain them?**

DISCUSSION

82. What rules of confidentiality govern consultations?

As with many law and mental health questions, there is no crystal clear answer. In *Tower v. Hirschhorn,* 397 Mass. 581 (1986), the SJC stated:

> We recognize that it is commonplace in the medical profession for physicians to consult with their colleagues regarding the treatment and diagnosis of patients within their care. This exchange of information is desirable, as it generally improves the medical care rendered. (588)

251 CMR 1.11 (see appendix A), which governs confidential communications for psychologists, provides that psychologists may consult with colleagues, with *or without* [italics added] client consent, when the pur-

pose of the consultation "is designed to enhance the services provided." 251 CMR 1.11 goes as far as to state that "the client's name or other identifying demographic information, or any other information by which the client might be identified by the consultant," may be disclosed to the consultant if, "in the psychologist's judgment, [such information is] necessary for the consultation to be successful."

The Law of No Surprises and the Parsimony Principle (see chapter 3) provide excellent guides here. It is enormously helpful if, during your first session, you inform your client about how you handle consultations, and then document that you have done so (see appendix B for a sample informed consent letter).

When you get the actual consultation, follow the Parsimony Principle: Be as precise as you can about what question you would like the consultant to answer, and then provide only the information necessary for the consultant to do the job. While only psychologists are provided explicit protection for divulging identifying information to a consultant, psychiatrists and other mental health professionals may do so *if it is necessary for the consultation to be successful.* To conclude otherwise would be tantamount to prohibiting clinicians other than psychologists from obtaining consultations, a result contrary both to the public policy stated in *Tower,* as well as to good clinical care. In addition, an exchange during your initial session may be considered to provide client consent for a consultation, and with such consent you may proceed.

83. From a professional liability perspective, what is the difference between a consultation and supervision?

The difference between a consultation and supervision lies in the degree to which an individual, other than a treater, becomes involved in and responsible for a treatment. This difference in degree has significant implications for liability.

A consultation consists of a treater bringing a specific question, or questions, to a consultant. A consultation is not open-ended or indefinite; the question is asked, a recommendation is made, and the treater is free to use the recommendation in whatever manner she feels will be most helpful to the treatment. The consultant assumes no responsibility for what the treater does, and makes a recommendation based only on what material the treater presents. When the consultant puts forth a recommendation, the consultant-consultee relationship ends. Because of the nature of this relationship, a consultant's liability is extremely limited. Consultants are rarely named as defendants in lawsuits.

A supervision consists of an ongoing relationship in which an entire treatment, or significant aspects of a treatment, are placed under the scrutiny of the supervisor. If the supervisee is a trainee, and the supervisor has both clinical and administrative responsibility for the supervisee's work, the supervisor is nearly as responsible for the treatment as if the patient were the supervisor's own. In this sense, the supervisor is much "closer" to the patient than is the consultant. If the supervisee is a licensed clinician with experience, the supervisor's responsibility is less, yet still considerably more than that of a consultant. A supervisor is responsible for actively exploring what the supervisee is doing, how the supervisee is handling the transference and countertransference, how she is addressing issues of safety, and the like. Because of their greater degree of involvement and responsibility, supervisors are much more likely to be named in a lawsuit than are consultants.

84. Is a trainee required to tell a patient that the treatment is being supervised?

Yes. Trainees must tell their patients that the treatment is being supervised.

85. What is negligent supervision? What would be an example of negligent supervision?

Negligent supervision is the failure to live up to the standard expected of you in the supervisory relationship. For this reason, it is important that you define the frame of the supervision at the outset. You will want to be clear about how often you and your supervisee will meet; which cases your supervisee will bring to the supervision; which aspects of those cases you will supervise; who, if anyone, will cover for you during vacations; and so forth. Once you set the frame, you will then be responsible for providing *reasonable* supervision. The important question from a professional liability point of view is: Given the frame, what would a reasonable supervisor do in these circumstances?

Andrews v. United States, a case in a federal court, provides an example of negligent supervision. Sandra Andrews went into therapy with Travis Gee, a physician's assistant with experience in counseling and psychology. Gee was supervised on the case by Dr. David Frost. A short while into the therapy, Gee told Ms. Andrews that she was suffering from chronic depression and that she needed an affair. Gee added that he was available. Under the guise of a therapy, Gee convinced Ms. Andrews to have intercourse. During the time Gee was sexually involved with Ms. Andrews, one of Dr. Frost's patients complained to Frost about Gee. Specifically, this patient told Dr. Frost that Gee had engaged in sexual activity with Ms. Andrews. In response, Frost confronted Gee. After Gee denied the allegations, Frost let the matter drop. Ms. Andrews' depression became much worse and, after she revealed to her husband what had occurred between her and Gee, her marriage ended. The former Mr. and Ms. Andrews then sued.

The federal court held that Frost's supervision of Gee had been negligent. The court reasoned that Frost had failed to "properly and promptly" investigate the allegations of sexual improprieties. From the court's point of view, Frost had failed to act *reasonably* as a supervisor. According to the court, a reasonable supervisor would have done more than simply ask Gee whether he was having sex with his patient, and then walk away when Gee said "No."

More mundane examples would be the following three. First, you have agreed to meet with your supervisee once per month, and you miss three months without taking the time to "check-in" with your supervisee. An untoward event happens. Your supervision could be considered negligent, because a reasonable supervisor would have made sure to communicate with the supervisee in some way about the status of the cases. Second, a supervisee talks at length about how physically attractive he finds his new patient. You do not address the erotic countertransference, nor do you attend to how the supervisee is handling the countertransference. An affair results. Your supervision could be considered negligent, because a reasonable supervisor would have made sure that the countertransference was appropriately addressed. Third, your supervisee begins to treat a patient with a long history of suicide attempts. For a period of several weeks you do not ask your supervisee about his assessment of the patient's suicidality, and the patient makes a serious suicide attempt. You could be considered negligent, because a reasonable supervisor would have made sure that the supervisee was adequately assessing the patient's suicidality. Your touchstone is what a reasonable supervisor would do under the circumstances.

86. Treaters often keep notes of their own countertransference fantasies, separate from the record. These are neither progress nor

process notes; their purpose is to help the treater gauge the nature and intensity of her own psychic processes as they relate to the clinical work. Could a lawyer ever obtain them?

They got Bob Packwood's diary. They can get your countertransference notes. When it comes to records or notes arising out of a treatment, the rule is: If the records exist, a lawyer can obtain them. While the records may not actually be introduced as evidence into a legal proceeding, at the very least they will be made available to a judge who will review them.

The records described in this question are the treater's personal notes. As such, they are not part of the record. The treater is not required to keep them and may dispose of them whenever she wishes *prior to receiving a subpoena*. Once the treater receives a subpoena—which will almost certainly call for "any and all" records —she is then obligated to ensure that *all* of her records remain intact until a decision is made about what material will be released. Many treaters believe that keeping a set of notes separate from the official record will insulate their notes from a subpoena. Not so. Whatever written materials arise out of a treatment may be requested—and possibly obtained—by a lawyer.

10

CONFIDENTIALITY, TESTIMONIAL PRIVILEGE, AND MANDATORY REPORTING

That we have both an entire chapter and a set of questions on the subject of confidentiality speaks to the importance of this topic to mental health professionals. The number of questions that can arise when a clinician is attempting to treat difficult or severely compromised patients is staggering; even the most routine work will inevitably raise dilemmas about when to release clinical material. The questions below are written as much for their content as for their demonstration of the process that should govern a treater's thinking when she is faced with the possibility of disclosing confidential information.

QUESTIONS DISCUSSED IN THIS CHAPTER

87. **What happens when a patient talks about having committed a crime in the past—or about intending to commit a crime in the future—that will not hurt anyone physically. Is there a duty to disclose this information?**

88. What happens to confidentiality and testimonial privilege when a patient dies?

89. In certain circumstances following a patient's death, the executor or administrator of the estate may waive privilege. What happens in actual practice following a patient's death, when the executor of an estate wants clinical records?

90. What is a mandated reporter?

91. I've heard that the mandatory reporting statute for children is relevant only when the abuse occurs at the hands of a caretaker—is this right? Does this mean that if an adult who is *not* a caretaker abuses a child, a clinician does not have an obligation to make a report? What if the abuser is another child?

92. Does this mean that if a child's neighbor—who is not a "caretaker"—is sexually abusing a child, you have no obligation under the mandatory reporting statute to make a report? What do you do in this case?

93. An extremely religious set of parents forbade me to break confidentiality when their 12-year-old child talked about having been sexually touched by a member of their clergy. The parents were adamant that this information was to go *nowhere*, or else I would never see the child again and face a lawsuit for breach of confidentiality. How best to handle this situation?

94. I'm a psychologist. Do I have an obligation to report *whenever* I have reasonable cause to suspect that a parent is abusing a child—even if my suspicion arises from what I see at the mall?

95. What should I do if a patient tells me that another treater has harmed her?

96. If I make a report under the mandatory reporting statute for children, can the child's parent—or the alleged perpetrator—find out that I was the one who reported?

97. I've heard that confidentiality works differently for groups than it does for individuals. Is this right?

98. Must a client be given some sort of warning before an evaluation is introduced into a legal proceeding?

99. What happens when a patient commits a crime against a mental health professional, say, by breaking into his therapist's office, or even by assaulting his therapist? Would confidentiality prohibit the therapist from bringing the matter to the police?

100. Could a lawyer ever obtain treatment records written by a rape crisis or domestic violence counselor, perhaps by claiming that the victim's records are necessary to defend his client in a criminal trial?

DISCUSSION

87. What happens when a patient talks about having committed a crime in the past—or about intending to commit a crime in the future—that will not hurt anyone physically. Is there a duty to disclose this information?

To answer this question, we look to the allied mental health and human services professional confidentiality statute (c.112, §172, in appendix A), and to the Massachusetts regulation governing confidential communications for social workers (258 CMR 22.01, in appendix A). The language in the statute and regulation is exactly the same: Licensed social workers, and allied mental health and human service professionals (licensed marriage and family therapists, licensed rehabilitation counselors, licensed educational psychologists, licensed mental health counselors), are not bound by confidentiality when the communication "reveals the contemplation or commission of a crime or a harmful act." The statute does not obligate these mental health professionals to disclose the communication; it says merely that they are not bound to keep such communications confidential. Four comments are in order.

First, this exception to confidentiality does not apply to psychologists, psychiatrists, or nurses. As a consequence, psychologists, psychiatrists, and nurses should treat information about past crimes in the same manner as they would treat any other information communicated in the course of a therapy. Confidentiality rules.

Second, the issue of future crimes—the "contemplation"—of a crime, is more complicated than the statute and regulation would suggest. Virtually all crimes entail the possibility of harm, either to a third party or to the perpetrator. Breaking into a home or apartment, for example, can place both the inhabitants and the individual entering at great risk. Stealing a car brings with it the possibility of a police chase, which could kill or injure the individual who stole the car, a police officer, or innocent bystanders. Whenever a client talks about committing a crime in the future, the treater should assess the degree to which harm is forseeable. If the crime is against the person or property of an identified third party, the treater should assess whether a duty arises under the *Tarasoff* statute (see chapter 2).

Third, a question arises whenever a treater listens to a client talk about a future crime: To what extent is the treater subtly encouraging—if only by failing to *discourage*—the client? Any action by a treater—before or after a crime—that could reasonably be viewed as encouraging, aiding, or harboring a criminal could be considered actionable by the police. When such material arises during the course of a therapy, the treater should be keenly aware of what posture she adopts. A consultation could prove invaluable.

Fourth, communications to social workers and allied mental health and human services workers about past or future crimes are not considered confidential under the statute and regulation, and so may not be protected by privilege. That is to say, if you are a member of these disciplines and you get called to court, your patient may not be able successfully to invoke testimonial privilege to prevent you from testifying about the "contemplation or commission" of a crime. The court will determine whether the exception to privilege applies; what's important is that you cannot assume this material will automatically be kept out of a legal proceeding because it was communicated during the course of a therapy.

88. What happens to confidentiality and testimonial privilege when a patient dies?

Confidentiality survives death. It is interesting, and perhaps a bit unfortunate, that only the psychology regulations (251 CMR 1.11, in appendix A) make this requirement explicit, "all communications . . . shall be deemed to be and treated as confidential *in perpetuity* [italics added]." Death does not untie or even loosen the bonds of confidentiality. *If a reason would not justify a disclosure of confidential information while your client was alive, it will not warrant a disclosure of confidential information after your client has died.* That said, you *do* release records if a court tells you to do so. If the administrator or executor of your patient's estate gives you permission to release the records, do so after obtaining a consult to ensure that releasing the records is ethically appropriate. You may legally release records in the latter circumstance because the administrator or executor is, in effect, standing in your patient's shoes. Before releasing any records, however, you will want to confirm the credentials of the administrator or executor in order to ensure that he truly is the representative of your patient's estate. If a spouse, child, or other family member requests records after a patient has died, you should (politely) explain that, while you would like to be as helpful as you can, you are not legally free to release those materials directly to him or her unless he or she has been appointed administrator or executor of the estate.

Testimonial privilege survives death as well. After your client dies, privilege passes to the executor of the estate, who then may decide whether to invoke privilege (prevent you from testifying or releasing records) or to waive privilege (allow you to testify or to release records). As an example of an instance in which an executor might want to waive privilege, consider a situation in which your client, shortly before her death, sold an extremely valuable piece of jewelry at a pawn shop for a fraction of its actual value, even though she was quite well-off and didn't need the money. Your client's family would like to establish that she was incompetent at the time she sold the jewelry, but it will be impossible to do so without your notes. In that instance the executor of the estate might agree to waive privilege and allow you to release records or to testify at a hearing, in order to help determine whether your client had been competent at the time of the sale. If she was not competent, the sale is not valid, and the jewelry returns to the estate.

Note that the testimonial privilege statutes for psychotherapists (c.233, §20B, in appendix A), and social workers (c.112, §135B, in appendix A) have an exception to privilege when a dead person's mental or emotional state is introduced at a legal proceeding. In such a case, a judge determines whether the exception applies to the case at hand. If the judges decides yes, she conducts an "in camera" review of the record (she reads it in her office), and then determines if anything in the record is relevant to the question before the court. The relevant portion of the record may then be disclosed. It is important to note that the exception to testimonial privilege is not automatic—the judge must first rule on its applicability and then review the record for relevance.

89. In certain circumstances following a patient's death, the executor or administrator of the estate may waive privilege. What happens in actual practice following a patient's death, when the executor of an estate wants clinical records?

Take the example above, where your patient, shortly before her death, sold a piece of jewelry for far below what it was actually worth. The executor of the estate has a duty to maximize the estate's value, and so may attempt to claim that your patient was not competent at the time of the sale. If a court agrees, the sale is not valid, and the jewelry returns to the estate.

The executor comes to you and asks that you release your treatment records. Suppose that the records contain information which you believe could be harmful to your patient's family, and may even color their memory of your patient. You decline to release the records. At this point the executor of the estate issues a subpoena "duces tecum," a subpoena that requires you to bring the records with you to court. You appear in court with the records and claim that confidentiality and privilege prevent you from releasing any information about the treatment. The executor points to the exception, found in the privilege statutes, which allows information to be released following a patient's death if the material is necessary to settle a legal claim. The judge then decides to conduct an "in camera" review. She takes your records, reads them in private, and determines what entries are relevant to your patient's competence at the time of the sale. She makes the relevant material available to the attorneys, for the purposes of settling the claim.

If, in the alternative, the records contained no information potentially harmful to the family, or to the memory of your patient, you may decide to release the records upon the executor's request, especially if you yourself had questions about the patient's competence at the time of the sale. In this case you would ask the executor for confirmation of her status, and then for a letter waiving privilege, signed by the executor in her capacity as executor of your patient's estate. (Your letter would follow the form in question 50.)

90. What is a mandated reporter?
A mandated reporter is any individual for whom the mandatory reporting statutes create a duty to report. Each mandatory reporting statute (see appendix A) lists a series of individuals who are required to make oral and written reports to the appropriate state agency when certain circumstances arise. These individuals are mandated reporters.

A mandated reporter who fails to make a report required by law is subject to a penalty. The statutes protect mandated reporters from a claim that they have breached a patient's confidentiality or privilege (see chapter 3).

91. I've heard that the mandatory reporting statute for children is relevant only when the abuse occurs at the hands of a caretaker—is this right? Does this mean that if an adult who is *not* a caretaker abuses a child, a clinician does not have an obligation to make a report? What if the abuser is another child?
The regulations governing the Department of Social Services are found in 110 CMR, the first part of which puts forth a series of definitions. "Abuse"

is defined in 110 CMR 2.00 as "the nonaccidental commission of any act *by a caretaker* upon a child under age 18" [italics in original]. "Caretaker" is defined as a child's parent, stepparent, guardian, any member of the household entrusted with a child's health or welfare, and:

> any other person entrusted with the responsibility for a child's health or welfare whether in the child's home, a relative's home, a school setting, a day care setting (including babysitting), a foster home, a group care facility, or any other comparable setting. As such "caretaker" includes (but is not limited to) school teachers, babysitters, school bus drivers, camp counselors, etc. The "caretaker" definition is meant to be construed broadly and inclusively to encompass any person who is, at the time in question, entrusted with a degree of responsibility for the child. This specifically includes a caretaker who is him/herself a child (i.e., a babysitter under age 18).

Note how expansive this definition is—any individual, regardless of age, who has any degree of responsibility for a child is considered a "caretaker." Abuse by such an individual requires a report.

If the individual alleged to have perpetrated the abuse falls unambiguously outside this circle, a report is not mandated by the statute. Nevertheless, our recommendation would be as follows: Whenever, in your capacity as a mental health professional, you receive information that gives rise to a reasonable cause to suspect child abuse, call the Department of Social Services. Explain the situation, and let DSS decide whether a report is necessary. If the DSS worker states that a report is required, defer to his or her judgment. Your report in this instance is made in good faith, and you are therefore protected from liability by the statute. If the individual with whom you speak indicates a report is not required, document your call by recording the time, date, name of the individual with whom you spoke, and the facts you provided that individual. You have then made a good faith effort to comply with the statute and may rely on the Department's judgment that no report is necessary. Remember that the individual at DSS will make a determination on the facts you provide; if you are incomplete in explaining the situation—even though you may be attempting to protect your client—you will defeat the purpose of your call and so cannot rely on the advice given.

One last point. Don't forget that the mandatory reporting statute for children also states that "neglect" is a reportable condition. Thus, if an older child is physically injuring a younger child, the adult caretaker may not be providing adequate supervision. In this case, you may be mandated to report because the caretaker has been neglectful.

92. Does this mean that if a child's neighbor—who is not a "caretaker"—is sexually abusing a child, you have no obligation under the mandatory reporting statute to make a report? What do you do in this case?

Although not mandated to make a report to the Department of Social Services, you would assess the degree of potential harm. If the child appears to be in imminent danger, you would convey your concerns to your patient and ask permission to discuss the matter with his or her parents. Lack of permission notwithstanding, you may give the information to a parent or guardian if you believe doing so is necessary to protect the child's safety.

If your patient is not in imminent danger, you should first discuss the matter with him or her in the treatment, and ask for permission to discuss the matter with the parents. In deciding whether to speak with the parents, you should take into consideration the child's age—the wishes of adolescents, for example, that you not take the matter outside the treatment would carry more weight. What to do in this instance rests upon your clinical judgment. It may also be helpful to keep in mind that sexual involvement with a minor is a crime. Although not reportable to DSS, a treater could certainly encourage a parent or caregiver to report the matter to the police.

93. An extremely religious set of parents forbade me to break confidentiality when their 12-year-old child talked about having been sexually touched by a member of their clergy. The parents were adamant that this information was to go *nowhere*, or else I would never see the child again and face a lawsuit for breach of confidentiality. How best to handle this situation?

Cases in which a disclosure of confidential information may end a therapy are especially difficult. Most poignant is that the victim—a child, and your patient—is made to suffer a second betrayal. Be that as it may, the law allows no room for discretion in this instance. Chapter 119, section 51A mandates you to report. You need not worry about a lawsuit; section 51A grants immunity to any mandated reporter who acts in good faith.

The Law of No Surprises may provide some help in cases like yours. If, in the first session, you review the exceptions to confidentiality, your response when disclosure becomes necessary can be along the lines of, "We've already had this discussion—legally, my hands are tied. The law simply allows me no option other than to report." While certainly no guarantee that the parents will allow their child to continue in therapy, this manner of handling the situation may provide enough distance for them at least to consider what would be in their child's best interests.

94. I'm a psychologist. Do I have an obligation to report *whenever* I have reasonable cause to suspect that a parent is abusing a child— even if my suspicion arises from what I see at the mall?

The mandatory reporting statutes are relevant only when you are acting *in your professional capacity.* If, on a Sunday afternoon trip to the mall, the zoo, or a museum, you happen to witness what you reasonably believe to be child abuse, you are under no obligation to report. You may, of course, choose to do so; reporting statutes provide that any individual acting in good faith may contact the appropriate state agency. No legal consequences will follow, however, if you do not.

To determine your obligation under the statute, ask yourself, "In what capacity have I received this information?" Put another way, the question is one of relevance—is your capacity as a mental health professional relevant to why or how you received the information? Say, for example, a reasonably reliable neighbor calls one evening and says, "I'm calling because you're the neighborhood psychologist and I want to know what to do; Sally Jones is being abused by her father." Even though Sally Jones is not your patient, you have received this information in your capacity as a psychologist and you now have an obligation to report. Or, as another example, you work at a mental health clinic and you overhear a parent threatening to scald her child with boiling water when they return home. Your professional capacity is relevant to how you received this information, and so you have an obligation to report. If you were to learn of either circumstance on a walk with your family, your professional capacity would not be relevant to how or why you received the information, and so you would not be a mandatory reporter.

95. What should I do if a patient tells me that another treater has harmed her?

This question is asked frequently, most often about a female patient who has been sexually involved with a male therapist. To answer the question, you must determine whether any mandatory reporting statute applies. If your patient is under 18, over 60, disabled, or in a residential facility, you may have an obligation to report the abuse. If your patient does not fall into one of these categories, however, you must have your client's consent before disclosing anything she tells you. While you can certainly advise your client of her options, for example that she may file a complaint with an ethics committee or a board of registration, without her consent you must keep the information confidential.

One note about reporting when the patient falls under the definition of a disabled person. Should the patient indicate that she does not want you to report—should she not consent to your disclosing confidential information—you are no longer a mandatory reporter. No penalty will attach if you do not make a report to the DPPC (see chapter 3).

96. If I make a report under the mandatory reporting statute for children, can the child's parent—or the alleged perpetrator—find out that I was the one who reported?

Chapter 110 of the Code of Massachusetts Regulations governs the Department of Social Services. 110 CMR 12.08 sets forth the conditions under which reports made pursuant to chapter 119, section 51A—the mandatory reporting statute for children—will be released. 110 CMR 12.08(5) states, "Whenever the Department releases any copy of a 51A report . . . the name of (and any other reasonably identifying data concerning) the reporter shall be redacted." A number of other regulations in chapter 110 provide that the name of the reporter will be redacted should the report be released. While no absolute guarantee can be given, the law has taken numerous steps to ensure that you cannot be identified as the individual who made the report. In the vast majority of cases this information will remain confidential.

97. I've heard that confidentiality works differently for groups than it does for individuals. Is this right?

Groups complicate confidentiality in several respects. First, by definition, conducting a group means that many clients are hearing information which, if said by a single client to a therapist, would be confidential. Second, there is no statute, regulation, or code of ethics that explicitly binds "patients" to confidentiality. Third, there is no statute or regulation that extends testimonial privilege to the members of a group.

Does this mean that confidentiality is strictly a clinical issue in group therapy? No. The right to privacy constitutes a legal constraint on what information citizens may share about each other. The Massachusetts privacy statute, M.G.L. chapter 214, section 1B, states in its entirety:

> A person shall have a right against unreasonable, substantial or serious interference with his privacy. The superior court shall have jurisdiction in equity to enforce such right and in connection therewith to award damages.

If citizen A, by sharing information about citizen B, creates an "unreasonable, substantial or serious interference" with B's right to privacy, citizen B can go into superior court and sue citizen A. Thus, members of a group are not free to share information from a group therapy with impunity; serious legal consequences can result. Because group members may not be protected by testimonial privilege, however, they could not necessarily rely on privilege to refuse to testify in a legal proceeding about what occurred during a group session.

98. Must a client be given some sort of warning before an evaluation is introduced into a legal proceeding?

Always be clear about who your client is. In this instance, know whether your client is *the court,* or whether your client is *the individual with whom you are speaking.* The difference is critical.

If your client is the court, you have an ethical obligation to make this fact known at the outset of an interview, before any clinical material is discussed. It makes no difference whether the proceeding is civil, criminal, or administrative in nature. The implication of having the court as a client is that information communicated during the course of meeting with the individual may be introduced into a legal proceeding. This must be explained, in terms understandable to the individual, before *any* other discussion takes place. If the individual begins speaking first, stop him. Your interruption has both an ethical and a legal purpose. Ethically, you must inform any individual with whom you meet in your capacity as a mental health professional of the limits to confidentiality. Legally, any material which has not been proceeded by this explanation, called a "Lamb warning," after *Commonwealth v. Lamb,* 368 Mass. 491 (1975), cannot be introduced into a legal proceeding. *If your client is the court, nothing matters until you have given a Lamb warning.*

If your client is the individual with whom you are speaking, you are bound by confidentiality and cannot testify unless your client waives privilege. The regular rules of confidentiality and testimonial privilege apply.

99. What happens when a patient commits a crime against a mental health professional, say, by breaking into his therapist's office, or even by assaulting his therapist? Would confidentiality prohibit the therapist from bringing the matter to the police?

No. The commission of a crime is outside the frame of therapy. A treater may report to the police the patient's name and facts about what occurred (for example, this individual broke into my office, and opened confidential files). A treater may not reveal anything about the nature, course, or content of the therapy, all of which are confidential. The fact of the crime, and the circumstances surrounding the crime, however, are not confidential.

100. Could a lawyer ever obtain treatment records written by a rape crisis or domestic violence counselor, perhaps by claiming that the victim's records are necessary to defend his client in a criminal trial?

This question has received much attention in Massachusetts, primarily because of how it lies at the crossroads of two important interests. On the one hand are the interests of criminal defendants. The Constitution provides that a criminal defendant has the right to information that could prove his innocence, as well as the right to confront those who accuse him of a crime. Innocent people are sometimes accused of crimes. On the other hand are the interests of victims of domestic violence and sexual assault. Victims of domestic violence and sexual assault need someone safe with whom to discuss what has happened. It was in recognizing the latter interests that the Massachusetts Legislature enacted M.G.L. chapter 233, sections 20J and 20K, the confidentiality statutes for sexual assault and domestic violence counselors (see appendix A).

In *Commonwealth v. Fuller*, 423 Mass. 216 (1996), and *Commonwealth v. Tripolone*, 425 Mass. 487 (1997), the SJC commented upon the reasons behind the absolute nature of confidentiality and testimonial privilege in the case of sexual assault or domestic violence. In *Fuller*, the SJC stated:

> By its terms, the privilege clearly promotes two important interests. First, it encourages victims of the brutal and degrading crime of rape to seek professional assistance to alleviate the psychological scarring caused by the crime, which may be more damaging than the physical

invasion itself. Second, the privilege supports the reporting of rapes, which . . . occur in considerable numbers, but frequently are not disclosed, because the victim may feel shame about the assault and may not be able to face the grueling nature of the adversary process that occurs at trial. (221–222, footnote omitted)

In *Fuller* and *Tripolone*, the SJC held that the absolute privilege, created by statute, will give way *only* when the criminal defendant's constitutional rights are compromised. To raise a constitutional issue, "the defendant must demonstrate a good faith, specific, and reasonable basis for believing that the records will contain exculpatory evidence that is relevant and material to the defendant's guilt" (*Tripolone* at 489, quoting *Fuller* at 226). If the defendant is able to demonstrate such a "good, faith, specific, and reasonable basis," the judge will review the records *in camera* (privately, in the judge's office). The crux of *Fuller* and *Tripolone* is that the absolute nature of the statutory privilege yields solely to the Constitution.

11

RECORDS AND RECORD KEEPING

Keeping records is an integral part of every mental health professional's work. Records provide an archive for what happened during an assessment or therapy, and are thus indispensable should care be transferred to another clinician. A record review is often an excellent way to help a therapy that has become "stuck" move forward. And a worthwhile consultation depends upon a reliable record. The law comes into play in a limited number of areas as, for example, in a lawsuit or action before a professional board, when an accurate record of what happened is essential, or when a patient wishes to see her records and the treater does not believe such a review will be in the patient's best interests. Below are questions that address situations in which the law touches upon this area of clinical practice.

QUESTIONS DISCUSSED IN THIS CHAPTER

101. Who owns a therapist's records?
102. What happens if a patient asks to see his or her records?
103. What if a patient believes part of the record is inaccurate and asks to have it changed?
104. What should a treater do with her records after retirement?
105. How long should a treater retain records?

DISCUSSION

101. Who owns a therapist's records?

The therapist owns the *physical document*, while the patient owns the *contents* of the record. The therapist's "ownership" of the records is subject to confidentiality and testimonial privilege. As a consequence, although the therapist owns the physical document, all of the laws of confidentiality, testimonial privilege, and mandatory reporting apply to how that ownership is exercised. Unless directed otherwise by statute or court order, the therapist can only do with the record what the patient authorizes.

102. What happens if a patient asks to see his or her records?

The answer to this question depends upon where the therapist works: in private practice apart from a hospital or clinic (private outpatient treatment), in a facility "under the supervision and control of or licensed by" the Department of *Mental* Health, or in a facility licensed by the Department of *Public* Health. Take private practice outside a hospital or clinic first; the relevant statute is M.G.L. chapter 112, section 12CC. Section 12CC provides that a patient or a patient's representative has the right to inspect the records. Note that the right is to *inspect*; the records themselves belong to you. If the patient wants copies, he must pay a "reasonable fee"; no fee, though, is required if the records are necessary to support a claim or appeal under certain benefit programs or the Social Security Act. Section 12CC of chapter 112 also states that a psychotherapist has the option of providing the patient either the *entire* record, or only a *summary* of the record "if in the reasonable exercise of his professional judgment, the psychotherapist believes providing the entire record would adversely affect the patient's well being." If, this judgment notwithstanding, the patient still wants to see the entire record, the psychotherapist must allow either the patient's attorney or a psychotherapist designated by the patient access to the record

For both clinical and risk management reasons, you should insist that you and your client review the record together. From a clinical perspective, the patient may encounter material that is unclear or troubling, and your presence will be important to address questions or concerns. From a risk management perspective, clients sometimes walk away with the record tucked under their arm. You are then deprived of your most important defense should the client make a claim against you. For this reason, a treater should __never__ provide a patient with the original record. A treater should either copy the record and allow the patient to review the copy, or the treater should review the record together with the client.

Access to records in facilities "under the supervision and control of or licensed by" the Department of Mental Health is governed by M.G.L. chapter 123, section 36 and 104 CMR 27.18. Section 36 of chapter 123 states that three situations warrant a patient's access to records: when a judicial order authorizes access, when the patient himself or through his attorney requests that the attorney have access to the records, and when the Commissioner, or someone designated by the Commissioner, determines that allowing access to the records would be in the patient's best interest. 104 CMR 27.18(6) gives several examples of the best interest rule: when the records are necessary to pursue or defend against a legal claim, to enforce a civil right, or to obtain third party payments.

Access to records in a hospital or clinic licensed by the Department of Public Health "not under control of the Department of Mental Health" is governed by M.G.L. chapter 111, sections 70 and 70E. Sections 70 and 70E make no distinction between psychiatric and any other records; all are grouped under the term "medical records." Section 70E(g) states that a patient has the right "to inspect . . . and to receive a copy" of his records. If the patient wants copies, he must, pay a "reasonable fee"; again, however, no fee is required if the records are necessary to support a claim or appeal under certain benefit programs or the Social Security Act.

103. What if a patient believes part of the record is inaccurate and asks to have it changed?

The clinical record is a legal document. You may not alter a legal document. "Altering" consists of making any change to what has been written; as examples, whiting out, blacking out, and crossing out all constitute altering the record.

That said, it sometimes happens that inaccuracies or mistakes in the record come to light. While you cannot alter the record, you also do not want to perpetuate inaccurate clinical information. If you become aware of a mistake in the record, you may make an additional entry. In the entry, reference the date of the mistaken information, explain that previously recorded information is inaccurate, provide the accurate information, and then date the entry according to when it is written. You may also make a notation next to the entry with the mistaken information, such as, "See note of September 18, 1997, for correction." Initial and date this

ACCESS TO RECORDS

I. Private, outpatient practice (apart from hospital or clinic)
    (M.G.L. c.112, §12CC)
    A. Patient has right to inspect records.
        1. Records belong to mental health professional.
        2. Patient must pay "reasonable fee" for copying.
        3. No fee required if records necessary for claims or
            appeals under certain benefits programs, or under the
            Social Security Act.
    B. Psychotherapist may provide "summary" of record if
        providing entire record deemed by the therapist not in
        patient's best interests.
    C. If patient requests entire record, notwithstanding
        psychotherapist's determination of "not in best interests,"
        entire record must be provided:
        1. To patient's attorney; or
        2. To another psychotherapist designated by patient.

II. Facility "under the supervision and control of or licensed by" the
    Department of *Mental* Health (M.G.L. c.123, §36; 104 CMR
    27.18). Access to records provided:
    A. Upon judicial order.
    B. Upon request that an attorney inspect records.
    C. When determined to be in "best interest of the patient,"
        e.g., to pursue or defend against a legal claim, to enforce a
        civil right, or to obtain third party payments.

III. Facility licensed by the Department of *Public* Health (not "under
     the control of" the Department of Mental Health) M.G.L. c.111,
     §§70 and 70E)
     A. No distinction made between medical and psychiatric
         records.
     B. Patient has right to inspect and receive copy of medical
         records.
     C. Patient must pay "reasonable fee" for copying.
     D. No fee required if records necessary for claims or appeals
         under certain benefits programs, or under the Social
         Security Act.

notation. In this manner you are adding correct information to, rather
than altering, the record.

It may happen that a patient brings to your attention a mistake in information that has been released to a third party. (The best preventative
medicine is to review the material with your patient *before* disclosure.) If
material is released, perhaps in the form of a letter, and your patient wants

a part of the letter corrected, you may send a second letter explaining that incorrect information was contained in the initial missive, and that the purpose of the second letter is to provide a correction.

104. What should a treater do with her records after retirement?
A treater who is retiring should keep two things in mind. First, the patient may continue to need mental health services, in which case the treater's records may play an important role in transferring care to another clinician. Second, a treater's retirement does not bar a patient from bringing a complaint or an action in malpractice. Notes may be crucial to the treater's defense.

After a treater retires, records should be retained in a safe, accessible location, so that patients who wish to continue with another treater may obtain copies. If the treater is moving to another location, she should: arrange to forward a copy of the records to patients, when clinically indicated; name another treater or responsible party to maintain the records in the event they are requested; provide the name of another treater or responsible party who will know how to reach the treater should a patient need a copy of the records.

105. How long should a treater retain records?
Certain disciplines specify a length of time treaters must keep records. The Board of Registration in Medicine, for example, requires a treater to maintain records for seven years following the last encounter. In addition, treaters must keep in mind that, according to the statute of limitations, children have three years from their 18th birthday, or until the age of 21, to bring a lawsuit (see question 19). If you treated a child when she was 4 years old, it would therefore be prudent to keep the records until she turned 21 (for 17 years).

Our recommendation is to keep records for a period of 10 years following termination. In the case of minors, keep the records 10 years following termination or until the child reaches the age of 21, whichever represents the longer period of time.

12

Professional Liability

Questions about professional liability are like fingerprints—no two are exactly alike. Change the facts, however slightly, and the answer will change as well. A lawyer's favorite phrase? "It depends . . ."

The responses below are best understood as providing ways to think about problems mental health professionals often face. They are not intended as definitive answers. When faced with your own dilemma, we have three recommendations: First, think carefully through your problem and consider alternative ways of responding as they present themselves; second, get a consultation; third, document your thinking and the consultation. Pay every bit as much attention to the process by which you come to your decision, and your documentation of that process, as you do to the decision itself.

QUESTIONS DISCUSSED IN THIS CHAPTER

106. Why do you place so much emphasis on documentation?
107. Should I continue to see a patient who is suing me?
108. What material should I be sure to cover during a first session?
109. Some clinicians actually give their clients an "informed consent" letter at a first session. Is this a good idea?

110. I serve as a med-backup for several non-MD therapists. To what extent could I be held liable for what goes on in these therapies?

111. Can you offer any guidelines as to when it is okay to accept a gift from a client, and when it is not?

112. I have a policy not to conduct a session with a patient who is under the influence of drugs or alcohol. Recently a client arrived at my office visibly intoxicated. When I said that we would not be having a session, he got back in his car and drove away. Would I have been liable had he gotten into a wreck?

113. Can I bill for a session I have refused to hold because the patient arrived at my office under the influence of drugs or alcohol?

114. What is my liability if a patient commits suicide?

115. Does a treater have a responsibility to report a patient who appears to be an impaired driver?

116. I'm semiretired and volunteer as a supervisor at a local mental health clinic. Given that I only do a few hours of supervision each week, need I worry about getting malpractice insurance?

117. Will my malpractice insurance pay for a lawyer to represent me on a complaint before a board of registration or professional society?

118. If I receive a letter of complaint from my board of registration, may I go ahead and respond?

119. What should a treater do when she receives a request for records from an insurance company?

120. If I'm sued, should I hire a personal attorney, in addition to the attorney the insurance company will provide?

121. What legal and ethical steps can a therapist take to terminate with a harassing or threatening patient?

122. I know that I am obligated to notify my insurance company if anything ever happens that might give rise to a malpractice lawsuit. Under what circumstances should I notify the company, and what is the best way to do the actual notification?

123. I've just received a managed care contract. Should I have a lawyer read it over?

124. Can a treater be held liable for not providing services a managed care company has denied?

125. What obligations does a researcher have when, during a research interview, a subject reveals information that would require a treater to act, for example, that the subject intends to hurt himself or someone else, or that a child is being abused or neglected?

126. **What are the concrete steps I can ethically and legally take to collect an unpaid fee?**
127. **Do you advise meeting with the family after a patient commits suicide?**
128. **Wouldn't saying that you are sorry be admitting that you did something wrong?**
129. **I've heard that there is a law creating public "profiles" for physicians. Can you explain exactly what the law does?**
130. **I am a psychiatrist who works for several nursing homes. Often I prescribe a low dose of an antipsychotic medication to settle a patient. Is this an acceptable practice?**
131. **What rules of confidentiality apply to patients who are sexually active and HIV positive?**

DISCUSSION

106. Why do you place so much emphasis on documentation?

Good clinical care requires thorough documentation, for many reasons. From the standpoint of professional liability, however, the matter can be summed up in seven words: *If it's not documented, it didn't happen.* Such is the import of *McNamara v. Honeyman*, 406 Mass. 43 (1989), in which the SJC allowed the plaintiff's expert to draw conclusions *solely from the record* about whether Dr. Honeyman had been negligent in treating Karen McNamara, a 20-year-old woman who committed suicide while in the hospital and under Dr. Honeyman's care.

Following Ms. McNamara's death, her parents sued Dr. Honeyman, claiming that his treatment of their daughter fell below the standard of care. Their expert, with the trial court's approval, testified that Dr. Honeyman's "failure to comport to good medical practice, *as documented*, contribut[ed] to her death" (at 59; italics not in original trial transcript). Several Justices of the SJC pointed out that the record did lack certain key elements, such as an admission history, a treatment plan, a review of prior records, regular observations of the patient, and notes about discussions with the staff. These Justices also pointed out, however, that "there was no evidence that Honeyman's performance was limited to whatever was recorded in the hospital charts" (at 60). Nevertheless, the majority of the Court let the expert testimony stand: Dr. Honeyman's care, *as reflected in the chart*, was negligent. The jury rendered a substantial judgment in favor of Ms. McNamara's estate.

107. Should I continue to see a patient who is suing me?

When a patient initiates an action against you—whether by submitting an ethics complaint or filing a lawsuit—the nature of your relationship with that patient has fundamentally changed. The frame of the therapy has shifted from words into action. While the change in your relationship will have clinical implications, the potential effects of the change extend *far* beyond the treatment. Your reputation, your income, and even your professional practice may be placed in jeopardy. Your personal life cannot remain unaffected. Only the extraordinarily rare mental health professional could keep an adequate handle on the countertransference under such circumstances, and we recommend that you not try.

First, the complaint or lawsuit will have to be talked about in the therapy—not to do so would constitute a major resistance for both the treater and the client. Talking about a pending lawsuit or complaint will inevitably evoke an intense reaction because your patient is attacking you—not with words, but with *actions*. No treater should place him- or herself under such a burden. Second, adding to this burden, any interpretation, recommendation, or suggestion you make to your patient immediately becomes suspect as flowing out of a countertransference reaction. You therefore have a higher standard to meet in explaining the reasons behind your work. Third, your legal bills are likely to accrue much faster than any fee your client is paying. You will thus be losing money while treating the client who is suing you. Doesn't sound like much fun to either of us.

You have no ethical obligation to continue treating a patient who has brought an action against you. You should arrange for an appropriate termination and ask for a consultation as the termination takes place. If you do decide to go ahead and treat a patient who has filed a complaint or lawsuit against you, it is essential that the treatment be supervised.

108. What material should I be sure to cover during a first session?

In the first session you should cover all the matters surrounding the "frame" of the therapy, that is, those aspects of your work that create the context in which the therapy takes place. The frame therefore includes the length of sessions, your per-session fee, whether you charge for missed sessions, whether you treat client vacations as missed sessions, whether you provide legal testimony, how you handle consultations and supervisions, whether you are available on an emergency basis, whether you accept phone calls at home, how often you bill, how you handle missed payments, what rules govern confidentiality, and the like.

What's important is to convey to the client a clear sense of how you work. The Law of No Surprises is relevant: A client should never be in a position of ignorance about the frame of the therapy.

109. Some clinicians give their clients an "informed consent" letter at a first session. Is this a good idea?

An informed consent letter has a number of advantages. First, such a letter makes clear the frame of the therapy. Second, an informed consent letter provides the client with a *physical* reminder of that frame, available whenever the client wishes to look at it. Third, it can be used to fulfill the legal obligation of psychologists and social workers to apprise clients "at the initiation" of the relationship of the rules concerning confidential information (see chapter 3). Fourth, it can provide an excellent reference when, into the therapy, you must disclose information for the purposes of a consultation or because a mandatory reporting statute requires you to do so: The possibility of disclosing information has already been addressed.

These advantages notwithstanding, many clinicians have very strong feelings that providing such a letter is *not* the way to begin a therapy. Our recommendation is to think through the advantages and disadvantages of an informed consent letter for your own practice, and proceed accordingly. One alternative to a letter would be a form, which many clinics and hospitals use, given to a client before, during, or immediately following the first session. Another alternative is to convey the information orally. In considering what will work best for you, keep in mind three things: First, you will be conveying a significant amount of information, more than most people can probably absorb in one sitting, especially when they may be feeling some anxiety; second, you are legally obligated to convey information about exceptions to confidentiality; and third, problems that arise in the course of a therapy often arise because a client had not been fully informed about some aspect of the frame.

If you decide to provide your client with an informed consent letter, we suggest you make a time, no later than the second session, to discuss any questions he may have about what is in the letter. Document that you have done so. From a professional liability point of view, it makes good sense to record in your notes at least one question the client has asked. Doing so illustrates that your client read the letter, and that you took the time to clarify questions he may have had.

A sample informed consent letter is included in appendix B.

110. I serve as a med-backup for several non-MD therapists. To what extent could I be held liable for what goes on in these therapies?

First and foremost, keep in mind *the nature of your duty*. As a med-backup, your duty is to provide reasonable care in prescribing medication. You will therefore take a history, do a physical, assess your patient's mental status, monitor side effects, and so forth. You will do these things because they are called for by the standard of care. Because you are not conducting a therapy, your duty does *not* extend to what care a reasonable therapist would provide. Nor does your duty extend to supervising the therapists for whom you act as med-backup. Thus, the nature of your relationship with the patient defines and limits your duty.

The situation becomes complicated when, for example, a patient tells you that he is suicidal during a routine check for medication side effects. Despite the complication, your duty remains defined by the nature of the relationship with your client. You will ask yourself what a reasonable med-backup would do in these circumstances. Your duty would be to assess the severity of the suicidal ideation, contact the patient's therapist, and make a plan with the therapist to ensure the client's safety. Be sure to document what you have done.

111. Can you offer any guidelines as to when it is okay to accept a gift from a client, and when it is not?

Unfortunately, there are virtually no hard and fast rules that govern the exchange of gifts between a mental health professional and a patient. Most often, the issue of gift giving arises in an ethics complaint; once the issue is raised, the burden shifts to the treater to show what therapeutic role the gift played. If the treater can show none, the exchange will almost certainly be seen as contrary to good treatment and therefore unethical. Accepting gifts of high monetary value (a piece of jewelry, a car) or of an intimate nature (a negligee, a card with clear sexual content) is always looked upon as unethical.

The most important principle to keep in mind is that for the vast majority of mental health professionals, words are the tools of the trade. Because the exchange of a gift is a communication, the mental health professional must ask herself what is being communicated and why the communication is not taking place in the currency of the profession, that is, with *words*. If you are faced with the dilemma of accepting, or giving, a gift, ask yourself the following three questions. First, does the gift comport with social convention? That is to say, is the gift of small or reasonable value, is the gift appropriate to a professional relationship, and does the exchange take place on an occasion that, in your patient's culture, calls for an exchange of gifts? Second, can the intrapsychic meaning of the gift be talked about in a manner appropriate to your patient's treatment? That is, can the communication be put into words and used to enhance or further your work, or at the very least to maintain the therapeutic alliance? Third, do you document the exchange? In other words, do you record the fact of the exchange itself, as well as your clinical assessment of what the exchange means to the patient, and what effect it will have on the treatment? If an exchange takes place, and your response to any of these questions is "no," get a consult. You're headed for troubled waters.

Finally, what you do with the gift is important. Placing cards and letters in the file shows that you are treating them as part of the therapy. Do not place birthday cake in the file. If the gift is a perishable item, there still may be a card that can be made part of the record. If the item is expensive, of an intimate nature, for example an article of clothing or jewelry, the only prudent path is not to accept the gift. The burden of explaining why you accepted the gift, should you be called by an ethics board to do so, will be virtually insurmountable.

112. I have a policy not to conduct a session with a patient who is under the influence of drugs or alcohol. Recently a client arrived at my office visibly intoxicated. When I said that we would not be having a session, he got back in his car and drove away. Would I have been liable had he gotten into a wreck?

This question provides an excellent example of when *the process by which you come to a decision* and the *documentation* of that process is every bit as important as the decision itself. Our response will therefore focus on the decision-making process.

First, consider whether the *Tarasoff* statute, chapter 123, section 36B (see chapter 2), is relevant. The statute requires you to act if your patient has expressed an "explicit threat" or if there is a "clear and present danger" toward an "identified victim." Although section 36B is probably not relevant to the situation you describe, pay attention to whether your patient has named any individual as the object of his anger as he walks away.

Next, consider chapter 123, sections 7 and 8. The complication with civil commitment under these sections is that mental illness is an essential element of the proceedings (see question 23) and alcoholism is expressly excluded from the definition of mental illness by 104 CMR 27.05 (see question 28). Do not, however, simply assume that the diagnosis of substance abuse precludes another diagnosis such as depression, which would warrant a pink paper. Consider the possibility.

A third alternative is chapter 123, section 35, which allows for commitment in virtue of substance abuse (see question 33). The standard for commitment under section 35 is that an individual's substance abuse creates "a likelihood of serious harm." Now, unlike the mandatory reporting statutes, section 35 doesn't actually require you to *do* anything, so—what next?

At this point in your decision-making process, you have two sets of legal principles which, given the circumstances, are in conflict—first, the principle that communications between you and your client are confidential, and second, the principle that individuals who present a danger because of their substance abuse and/or mental illness may be civilly committed in order to attenuate that danger. We place these principles in the context of the Law of No Surprises—to the extent practical and appropriate, any disclosures should be done together with the client—and the Parsimony Principle—disclosure is kept to the absolute minimum needed to achieve your goal. How is our balancing act put into practice?

Begin by discussing the dilemma with your patient, "We won't be meeting, but you're in no shape to drive. What other arrangements can we make?" Other arrangements may be having your client sit in your waiting room with a cup of coffee, contact a friend or relative for a ride, take a bus or other public transportation, or call a cab. Each of these alternatives represents a way to work with your client that entails a minimum of disclosure. By considering and raising these possibilities, you are demonstrating to anyone who reads the chart that you are approaching a difficult situation in a thoughtful, clinically appropriate manner.

If your client refuses your suggestions and insists on getting in his car, you then indicate that given the dangerousness of the situation, you may need to contact some authority. What allows you to take this next step is that all your suggestions for a *less* intrusive intervention have been rejected. If you now decide to contact the police and indicate that an intoxicated individual is driving down Route 2, you have protected yourself from a claim that your disclosure was premature, unwarranted, or more than necessary. Note that even this release is minimal—your "disclosure" is limited to a description of the client's car and perhaps a license plate number. You have acted because your client's substance abuse is creating "a likelihood of serious harm" and no intervention short of disclosing this information to the police is sufficient to attenuate the danger.

Keep in mind that every bit as important as what you eventually decide to do is the process by which you make your decision and your documentation of that process.

113. Can I bill for a session I have refused to hold because the patient arrived at my office under the influence of drugs or alcohol?

If you're asking this question when it comes time to write your bills, you're asking too late. You may bill for the session, not bill for the session, or reschedule the session, without concern for unwanted repercussions, *provided you made your policy clear at the beginning of your work.* Trouble will arise not from what you decide to do, but rather from failing to have a treatment agreement that tells your client what you will do under these circumstances. If you intend to work with patients who struggle with substance abuse, it is wise to include your policy in an informed consent letter (see appendix B).

114. What is my liability if a patient commits suicide?

No behavior can be predicted with absolute certainty. Suicide is a behavior. Suicide cannot be predicted with absolute certainty.

The task a mental health professional faces with a suicidal patient is not to predict whether the patient will commit suicide; rather, the task is to assess the *likelihood* that the patient will commit suicide. In assessing the likelihood that a patient will commit suicide, the clinician examines factors in the individual's life associated with a *greater* risk of suicide, factors associated with a *lesser* risk of suicide, and how the factors compare with one another. Lest this analysis seem overwhelming, consider that you do much the same thing each time you debate whether to carry your umbrella out the front door. You identify factors associated with a greater risk of rain (rain is predicted; it's windy; it's raining to the west) and factors associated with a lesser risk of rain (the sun is out; it's August). You then balance the factors against one another and decide whether to take your umbrella.

The crucial part of a suicide assessment is identifying those factors that speak to the likelihood that your patient will commit suicide. Examples of factors associated with a greater risk of suicide include a history of suicide attempts, the intent to commit suicide, a plan to commit suicide, the means to carry out the plan, feelings of hopelessness, a panic disorder, a delusion that suicide is a way to join a loved one who has died, social isolation, current or chronic substance abuse, a history of suicide in the family, and a belief that suicide is "fated." Examples of factors associated with a lesser risk of suicide include plans for the future, religious convictions that prohibit suicide, living with another person or persons, a sense that someone or something still endows life with meaning, and a belief that feelings of sadness, loss, or hopelessness are temporary and will pass.

In assessing the likelihood that an individual will commit suicide, you will therefore explore factors associated with greater and lesser risks of suicide, examine how the factors you have identified compare with one another, decide what to do based upon the comparison, and document the reasons behind your decision. *What protects you from liability is <u>not</u> that you have made the "right" decision, but your documentation of a process—the process by which you have assessed and responded to the likelihood that your patient would commit suicide. Your documentation should answer three basic questions: What did I do? Why did I do it? On what basis did I reject alternative ways of responding?*

115. Does a treater have a responsibility to report a patient who appears to be an impaired driver?

In Massachusetts, there is no mandatory reporting law for impaired driving. So, in thinking about this question, keep in mind where a treater's competence lies. A treater is competent in the diagnosis, assessment, and treatment of mental and emotional problems. A treater is not competent to diagnosis, assess, or treat a patient's difficulties with navigating the Massachusetts Turnpike at rush hour. The Department of Motor Vehicles is. *A treater should never assess whether an individual is competent to drive—assessing that competence is outside the treater's competence.*

If you have reason to believe that a patient's driving presents a danger, take three steps. First, identify what is creating the danger; second, consider what obligation you may have to address the danger; third, consider how best to fulfill your obligation. If, for example, your patient names an individual whom he intends to harm by "driving them off the road," chapter 123, section 36B, the *Tarasoff* statute, comes into play. In this case the car is the means of harm, and you would handle the situation in the same manner you would if the patient threatened to shoot someone. What's important in creating your duty is not the means by which your patient intends to do harm (driving someone off the road), *but your patient's intent to do harm.* As another example, if your patient has become grossly psychotic and insists on driving in an acute paranoid state, chapter 123, sections 7 and 8 may be relevant. You would determine whether your patient creates a likelihood of serious harm because of his mental illness. Again, what's relevant is not the car, but rather that your patient is engaging in an activity which, because of his mental illness, is dangerous. Your obligation would be the same if he were climbing trees while under the delusion that he could fly. As a third example, your patient may be dangerous because he is driving while drunk. In this case chapter 123, section 35 could be relevant, if your patient creates a "likelihood of serious harm," by his alcohol abuse. Your legal duty would be no different were he to drink and engage in any other dangerous activity, such as cutting down trees with a chain saw. *In each case focus not on the driving, but on the dangerousness and the source of the dangerousness, that is, intent to harm, mental illness, or substance abuse.*

Once you have determined whether you have an obligation to act, consider how best to fulfill that obligation. The place to start is always with the patient: Address the matter directly, convey your concern, and make a plan. Consider what assistance or support family or friends can provide. If necessary, insist to your patient that everyone sit down together. External constraints, such as the police, are available, but should be used only when all else fails.

116. I'm semiretired and volunteer as a supervisor at a local mental health clinic. Given that I only do a few hours of supervision each week, need I worry about getting malpractice insurance?

The necessity of obtaining malpractice insurance depends neither upon the number of hours you work nor upon how much you are paid. Once you establish a professional relationship with a supervisee, you are held to a standard of care. If you fall below that standard, you can be held negligent, and so responsible for any damages that result from your negligence.

In volunteering as you do, you are establishing a professional relationship with your supervisees. (Don't be fooled—the word "professional" in this context does not refer to salary nor to a full-time position. "Professional" refers to a relationship based upon your experience and expertise as a trained clinician.) You need malpractice insurance as much as does any other supervisor at the mental health clinic.

One final note for MDs: By statute you are required to carry malpractice insurance if you are engaged in active practice. Supervision is active practice. If you work part-time you may obtain malpractice insurance at a reduced rate.

117. Will my malpractice insurance pay for a lawyer to represent me on a complaint before a board of registration or professional society?

Some malpractice carriers will insure you for up to $5,000 in legal expenses for representation before administrative agencies such as boards of registration and professional societies. You should review your general malpractice policy to determine whether this coverage is included.

If a complaint is filed against you before a board of registration, be sure to find a lawyer who has experience before regulatory boards. The reason is that, in a great many cases, a complaint will be dismissed at the initial stage if the response is well-written.

118. If I receive a letter of complaint from my board of registration, may I go ahead and respond?

You need to exercise a good deal of caution when answering a letter from a board of registration. The board will ask you to produce certain materials, along with a letter responding to the allegations. Your response may require you to disclose confidential material. *A complaint to a board of registration or professional association by a patient does not, in and of itself, grant the authority to discuss the patient's case or to release the patient's records. The patient must first sign a release. If you disclose confidential information to the board without a release, you risk another complaint against you—for breach of confidentiality.*

A sample reply letter to a board of registration is contained in appendix B. It is best to send the letter by certified mail, return receipt requested, thus obtaining written confirmation that the board has received your letter.

If you subsequently do receive a release from the patient, it makes good sense to contact your malpractice carrier, whose claims representative should help you draft a letter in response to the allegations. The reason contacting the carrier is a good idea is that your response to the board is subject to discovery, which means that the other side in a lawsuit can obtain your response if the case goes to trial. For this reason, what you say in the letter can be extremely important, both in the matter before the board and in future litigation.

119. What should a treater do when she receives a request for records from an insurance company?

Whenever a treater receives a request for records from an insurance company, the treater should discuss the request with the patient. *Do not simply rely on the fact that the insurance policy contains a clause allowing for a release of records—the request must be discussed with the patient before you do anything.* It is well within a patient's prerogative to forego insurance benefits, and you should have a written release from your patient before you comply with an insurance company's request for records.

In terms of what records to release, an insurance company is entitled to so much of the record as is necessary to determine whether the treatment is consistent with the diagnosis. This information would include, for example, diagnosis, prognosis, dates of treatment, and length of treatment sessions. An insurance company is not entitled to process notes, which should be released only when your patient gives specific permission to do so. If the request for records concerns treatment that falls under the $500 outpatient benefits for mental illness, general accident and sickness policies, health maintenance organizations, preferred provider arrangements, and medical service corporations doing business in Massachusetts are only entitled to the patient's name, the *DSM* diagnoses, and the date and type of service provided.

120. If I'm sued, should I hire a personal attorney, in addition to the attorney the insurance company will provide?

A personal attorney is an attorney of your own choosing, whom you will pay out of your own pocket. There are three ways in which a personal attorney could be helpful if you are sued. First, litigation is enormously stressful. A lawsuit has the potential to invade all areas of your life, personal as well as professional, and involves people, places, and events that will feel foreign and hostile. A personal lawyer can be helpful in shepherding you through the process, explaining how things will work, and calming your anxieties. The attorney assigned by the insurance company may fill this role, but not necessarily.

The second way in which a personal attorney can be helpful is to be mindful of how your interests may diverge from the interests of the insurance company. The attorney assigned by the insurance company will pursue the company's interests; most often, but not always, these will coincide with your interests. Examples of times when the insurance company's interests may differ include when the insurance company would prefer to settle and you want the case to go forward, or when the insurance company is representing more than one defendant in a single lawsuit. In the latter case the company will want to minimize its *total* losses, which will not necessarily entail minimizing *your* losses. A personal lawyer can be helpful in watching for these and other situations where the interests of the insurance company differ from your own.

The third way in which a personal attorney can be helpful is that, unbeknownst to many clinicians, a malpractice policy may include a "consent to settle" clause. Such a clause requires the carrier to obtain your written consent before settling the case. Your own attorney can review your policy for such a clause, discuss the pros and cons of settling if the issue arises, and deal with the carrier should there be any difference of opinion.

For these three reasons, it may well be worth the expense to hire a personal attorney as a consultant during a malpractice suit. You will want an attorney who is experienced in malpractice litigation, particularly on the defendant's side. Keep in mind that the attorney from the insurance company, not your personal attorney, is managing the case, and work to avoid any conflicts between them. That said, your own personal attorney, with whom you can "check in" as you feel the need, and who will have only your interests at heart, can be an important asset during the often long and always tumultuous experience of a lawsuit.

121. What legal and ethical steps can a therapist take to terminate with a harassing or threatening patient?

When facing the need to terminate with a difficult patient, a treater should keep two points in mind. First, a therapist is not required to treat every patient. The choice about whom to treat belongs *to the treater*. Second, termination is *not* the same as abandonment. The second point bears elaboration.

Abandonment can be described as an inappropriate termination. Examples of abandonment are terminating a treatment without notice, without regard for the patient's condition at the time of termination, without an adequate plan for follow-up treatment, or in order to retaliate against a patient. *A treater may not abandon a patient.*

Termination is a process, which the circumstances of a treatment may demand. Termination may be appropriate because a therapy is no longer in a patient's best interests. Perhaps, for example, the patient is treatment resistant, has continuously missed sessions, or often comes to appointments under the influence of drugs or alcohol. Termination may also be appropriate because the patient has intruded upon the therapist's private life, has violated a professional boundary such as by breaking into the therapist's office, or has threatened the therapist. *While a treater may not abandon a patient, a treater may terminate with a patient.*

When termination with a difficult patient is appropriate, what becomes important is *the process by which the termination takes place.* We find it helpful to break this process down into five parts, which may occur sequentially or simultaneously, depending upon the circumstances. First, discuss the difficulty with the patient and explain that, if change does not occur, termination will result. Be clear about what changes must occur, in a way that can be measured and documented. Second, if termination is or becomes the only alternative, explain to the patient why you are terminating and offer termination sessions (usually between one and three), unless precluded by the patient's behavior. Third, obtain a consult to maintain your objectivity and to review whether you are proceeding appropriately. Fourth, to the extent possible, provide the patient with the names and telephone numbers of other treaters in the area. If your patient refuses the referrals, inquire why and then document both the refusal and your patient's reasons. (If your patient is in crisis, the responsibility will be yours to ensure that another treater is immediately available and to consider whether a hospitalization is appropriate. If other treaters are not immediately available, you will need to delay the termination until the crisis has abated.) Fifth, document your reasons for termination and your plan for referral. Send a letter to your patient with this information, and place a copy of the letter in the patient's record.

A sample letter of termination is included in appendix B.

Not all terminations go smoothly. Some patients will resist, and then claim abandonment and threaten to sue or file a complaint with your licensing board. The more difficult you expect the termination to proceed, the more attention you should give to outside consultations and proper documentation.

122. I know that I am obligated to notify my insurance company if anything ever happens that might give rise to a malpractice lawsuit. Under what circumstances should I notify the company, and what is the best way to do the actual notification?
Insurance companies require notice from treaters whenever a threat of a lawsuit arises, for several reasons. First, the insurance company will want

to review the problem, decide whether something must be done, and assign the matter to an attorney for further action if called for. Second, if the insurance company decides the matter does warrant action, the company's attorney will be in touch with the treater, to make sure that the treater does not make any statements that could negatively affect the lawsuit. Third, certain legal papers require a response within a defined period of time. A "93A" claim, for example, must be answered within 30 days. A summons and complaint has a 20-day requirement. The insurance company will want to make sure that responses are timely.

In regard to the actual notification, a treater should contact the insurance company whenever there is a reasonable basis to believe that a lawsuit is a possibility. The following circumstances would therefore warrant notification: The treater receives a summons and complaint for a lawsuit; a treater receives a 93A letter; a treater receives a letter from a lawyer representing a present or former patient, stating the patient's intent to bring a lawsuit; a treater receives a letter from a present or former patient, or a lawyer representing a present or former patient, requesting a copy of the treatment record, and something has happened in the treatment that might give rise to a complaint or lawsuit; some event occurs during the course of a treatment that a reasonable person would assume could lead to a complaint or lawsuit—examples of such an occurrence would be a suicide, a homicide committed by a patient, or a patient complaint that the treater breached confidentiality.

There is no "right" way to notify the insurance company. The best way to begin is to call the carrier, ask to speak with a claims representative, and explain the situation. If the claims representative says that the matter is not something the company would address at present, make a note of the date, the time, and the name of the representative. If the claims representative says that the company will want to deal with the situation, send the company any documents you have received, along with a cover letter that notes the date and time you initially made contact with the company.

123. I've just received a managed care contract. Should I have a lawyer read it over?

When most therapists receive a managed care contract they sign it, return it to the managed care company (MCC), and file their copy away for future reference. The next time they look at the contract is to read it— usually for the first time—when a problem arises. At that point they discover that the "one-year contract" may be canceled with 60 days notice for no reason at all. This is just one of several reasons why you should never sign a managed care contract without carefully reading it through with an experienced attorney. The following are four additional examples of why it is good to be familiar with a managed care contract before you sign.

Most contracts contain some sort of *indemnification clause.* An indemnification clause requires a therapist to reimburse the MCC for losses or expenses that arise from a claim or lawsuit, if the loss or claim results from the therapist's participation in the contract. The therapist's malpractice insurance will probably not cover the cost of the reimbursement. The reason is that most malpractice insurance covers only actions in negligence, not actions based in contract, which is what an action arising from an indemnification clause will be. The wording of an indemnification clause is important, and most MCCs will work with a treater to alter the wording. The advice of an attorney as you work with the MCC is worthwhile.

Most contracts stipulate *duties the therapist owes to the MCC that are for the benefit of the patient.* MCCs will usually require that a therapist be available to see patients at specific times for emergencies. MCCs may also require the therapist to be available 24 hours a day, both by beeper and by "live" telephone coverage. Almost always the therapist will be required to cover for other therapists. All such contractual agreements with the MCC are for the "benefit" of the patient. If you fail to fulfill one of these requirements, and a patient comes to harm as a result of your failure, a lawsuit may ensue. It is therefore essential that you become familiar with the clinical responsibilities required by the contract.

Most contracts require a therapist *both to maintain patient confidentiality and to provide the MCC with access to and copies of all treatment records.* These two requirements often conflict, and it is important to have some resolution before beginning work under the contract. The reason a resolution is important is that your agreement with the MCC is not binding on the patient. Confidentiality belongs to your patient, who must consent before you release records to the MCC. Make this clear with the MCC before beginning to treat patients.

A therapist has *a duty to appeal a decision to deny services when the therapist believes the services are medically necessary.* When an MCC denies a service because, in the opinion of the MCC, the service is not medically necessary, a therapist has a duty to appeal the MCC's denial.

Such an appeal may create an uncomfortable situation for the therapist, insofar as she will be appealing a decision of the company who is paying her. The therapist's failure to appeal, however, could lead to a claim of abandonment, especially if the therapist believes that the denied service *is* medically necessary. Regardless of the MCC's decision not to fund, the therapist must be careful not to stop treatment if she believes stopping would be harmful to the patient. If the therapist does decide to stop treatment, she may do so only when the patient is stabilized, and only after she has referred the patient to other treaters.

These five examples—many more could be provided—illustrate the importance of having an attorney read over a managed care contract before you sign.

124. Can a treater be held liable for not providing services a managed care company has denied?

An MCC's decision to deny services will not in any way protect a therapist from a claim of negligent treatment or abandonment. A therapist must provide care that is "reasonable." Care that falls below what is reasonable, regardless of an MCC's decision to deny services, may be considered negligent and may give rise to an action in malpractice.

A treater's obligation to provide reasonable care and an MCC's decisions about what treatment to fund are entirely separate. Linking the two is asking for trouble. If a treater believes that an MCC will not fund care that is reasonable, and the treater wishes to stop treatment, the termination must be handled in the same manner as any other termination (see question 121).

125. What obligations does a researcher have when, during a research interview, a subject reveals information that would require a treater to act, for example, that the subject intends to hurt himself or someone else, or that a child is being abused or neglected?

Once again, this question has no straightforward answer. Perhaps the best advice we could give in this situation would be to follow the Law of No Surprises: When conducting research that is likely to uncover information that would create a duty to act were you a treater and your subject a patient, state explicitly how this situation will be handled in your informed consent form. Use your clinical judgment about what material your survey, interview, or questionnaire is likely to pull for. Once you've made that judgment, be up front about what you will do if such a situation arises. You may have concerns about whether your subject will be as forthcoming for your research; being up front at the outset, however, will save you much angst and spare your subject the feeling that you have betrayed a confidence you promised you'd keep.

That said, let us consider each of the examples in the question. First, a researcher should make an effort to ensure the safety of a patient who communicates a serious threat to harm himself. This effort could take a number of forms. If, for example, the research is being conducted at a hospital, the researcher should notify the unit staff. If the research is being conducted on an outpatient basis, the researcher should notify the individual's outpatient clinician, immediately if the circumstances warrant. If the research is being conducted on an outpatient basis, and the subject does not have an outpatient clinician, then a researcher who is licensed in one of the professions that may sign a pink paper (see question 31) would be well advised to make a reasonable effort to hospitalize the research subject.

Second, the Massachusetts *Tarasoff* statute, chapter 123, section 36B, states that a duty arises when a "patient' makes certain communications. If, however, someone gets hurt, the distinction between a "subject" and a "patient" may not hold sway over a jury, especially if the researcher is a mental health professional, as defined by M.G.L. chapter 123 (see chapter 2). The prudent course would be to warn, or take some other protective measure, if a patient makes a communication that would fall under section 36B. The subject may bring a complaint for breach of confidentiality, but such a complaint would be given little merit.

Third, chapter 119, section 51A, the mandatory reporting statute for children, makes no mention of the relationship between the parties. If the researcher is listed as a mandatory reporter and she is acting in her professional capacity—which she will be, when conducting research—she is mandated to report whenever she has "reasonable cause to suspect."

126. What are the concrete steps I can ethically and legally take to collect an unpaid fee?

You have no ethical duty to treat a patient who does not pay you, and you may terminate in an appropriate manner as you initiate proceedings to collect your fee. Moreover, both the confidentiality and testimonial privilege statutes (see chapter 3) provide for disclosure sufficient to allow such proceedings to move forward. Nevertheless, attempting to pursue legal means to collect a fee will likely cause you more trouble than it's worth.

Your legal bills for collecting the fee will almost certainly surpass—perhaps substantially so—the fee itself, and your attempts to collect the fee may create fertile (albeit unfounded) ground for an ethics complaint, the only basis for which may be the patient's rage at what's going on.

Our recommendation is that you bring the matter up with your client. Assess the client's ability to pay; virtually all clients will be able to pay *something*. Then determine what sort of free-care component your practice can allow. If you are able to accommodate your client's financial situation, work out a payment schedule and offer the client a reduced fee. If you are not able to accommodate your client's financial situation, arrange for an appropriate transfer of care to a low-fee clinic. Give serious thought to forgiving a debt that your client says she cannot, or refuses, to pay. Attempting to collect may bring trouble that far outweighs any moneys you would eventually receive.

The best way to avoid this problem is to make clear to your client your policy about late or missed payments. *Payment for your services is as much a part of therapy as therapy itself; late or missed payments, if not addressed in a clear, direct manner, will inevitably be disruptive to your work.*

See the sample informed consent letter in appendix B.

127. Do you advise meeting with the family after a patient commits suicide?

Meeting with a family after a patient commits suicide is like sailing between the Scylla of family grief and the Charibdis of confidentiality. Many clinicians feel an instinct to avoid any contact whatsoever with the family; most often these clinicians use confidentiality as a reason for not doing so. For the reasons explained below, we recommend that you accommodate the family's wishes in this regard.

First, meeting with the treater may be part of the family's process of grieving. In many instances, the treater is the individual who knows most about what was going on in the patient's life, and merely sitting with that individual can provide comfort to many families. Second, a meeting affords the opportunity for the treater personally to express her grief to the family and to tell the family how sorry she is about their loss. Hearing the treater speak these words in their presence can be an enormous service to many families. Third, while confidentiality must be maintained, confidentiality places no constraint on the treater listening to what the family has to say about their own feelings of loss, anger, and confusion. Although a treater may not reveal what was said during sessions, she may paint with broad brushstrokes issues salient in the patient's life, "We know he had been struggling with depression for many years," "Feelings of anxiety made it difficult for him to enjoy things he had enjoyed in the past." Fourth, perhaps more from a risk management point of view, suspicions or paranoia about whether a treater is responsible for a patient's death will only be enhanced by a refusal to meet.

Our recommendation would be to tell the family that you are very sorry for their loss, and then inquire whether they would like to meet with you. Your inquiry should be inviting, "Many families have found that meeting with the treater helps." You need to be clear that, while you will not be free to discuss any details about your work, you are very interested in hearing what the family is experiencing. (See also the following question.)

128. Wouldn't saying that you are sorry be admitting that you did something wrong?

Massachusetts has what is called an "apology statute." An apology statute allows a treater to offer an expression of sympathy without fear that her kind or sympathetic words may later be used against her in a lawsuit. M.G.L chapter 233, section 23D states:

> Statements, writings or benevolent gestures expressing sympathy or a general sense of benevolence relating to the pain, suffering or death of a person involved in an accident and made to such person or to the family of such person shall be inadmissible as evidence of an admission of liability in a civil action.

You may tell a family that you are terribly sorry about their loss, that what has happened is awful, that they have suffered an enormous tragedy, that their pain must be very deep. All of these fall within the statute and cannot be used against you. If, however, you add that your screw-up *caused* the family's loss, you have then made what is called a "statement against interest," which can (and very likely will) be used against you at trial.

129. I've heard that there is a law creating public "profiles" for physicians. Can you explain exactly what the law does?

The law, M.G.L. chapter 112, section 5, directs the Board of Registration in Medicine to make available to the public certain information about physicians licensed by the Commonwealth. There are three things you should note about the law: what information is made available to the public, what disclaimers must accompany information contained in the profile, and what protections are afforded against incorrect information being disseminated to the public.

First, the statute provides what is best described as a laundry list of information for an individual profile to contain. This information includes any of the following that have occurred within the past ten years: serious criminal conviction, final board disciplinary actions, revocation or restriction of hospital privileges for reasons of character or competence, and payments for medical malpractice court judgments, arbitration awards, or settlements. Anything occurring more than ten years ago is not covered by the law. Pending malpractice claims are also not made part of the profile. In addition, the profile indicates where the physician went to medical school and when she graduated, what postgraduate training she received, her special board certifications, and the names of hospitals where she has privileges. The physician may choose whether she wishes the profile to contain information about faculty and teaching appointments in the past ten years, publications in peer-reviewed journals within the past ten years, professional and community services and awards received for those services, where she primarily practices, whether there are translation services at her primary site, and whether she participates in the Medicaid program.

Second, the law states that malpractice settlements must be accompanied by a disclaimer. The disclaimer states:

> Settlement of a claim may occur for a variety of reasons which do not necessarily reflect negatively on the professional competence or conduct of the physician. A payment in settlement of a medical malpractice action or claim should not be construed as creating a presumption that medical malpractice has occurred.

Thanks, guys. That helps a lot.

Finally, the law states that the Board must provide a physician with a copy of her profile before releasing it to the public. The law also stipulates that the physician be given a reasonable time to correct any factual inaccuracies.

130. I am a psychiatrist who works for several nursing homes. Often I prescribe a low dose of an antipsychotic medication to settle a patient. Is this an acceptable practice?

Many psychiatrists follow this practice. When doing so, however, be sure to follow the letter of the law, for the reasons explained below.

First, every adult client is entitled to informed consent concerning treatment (see question 65). If you question whether a patient can give informed consent, you must assess that patient's competence to do so.

Second, the Massachusetts Attorney General has adopted a regulation with the following provision: It is an "unfair" and "deceptive" act for a nursing home administrator or licensee to treat a patient with antipsychotic medications without first obtaining a competent patient's written informed consent, or obtaining a Rogers order for an incompetent patient. Note that this regulation merely restates the law. By using the words "unfair" and "deceptive," however, the Attorney General's regulation *triples* the amount a patient could win in a lawsuit. This regulation has significantly upped the ante.

Bottom line: Be sure to obtain informed consent from your patients. If a patient is not competent to give informed consent, obtain a Rogers order, or inquire whether there is a health care proxy available to obtain consent (see question 79).

131. What rules of confidentiality apply to patients who are sexually active and HIV positive?

This question provides another excellent illustration of how the process by which you come to a decision and your documentation of that process are every bit as important as the decision itself.

The sexually active, HIV positive patient creates a bind for the mental health professional because of two conflicting obligations. The first obligation, arising from M.G.L. chapter 111, section 70F, is the duty to keep HIV status confidential, which is explicit and absolute: "No health care facility . . . and no physician or health care provider shall . . . disclose the results of [the HIV] test to any person other than the subject thereof without first obtaining the subject's written informed consent."

The second obligation arises from M.G.L. chapter 123, sections 7 and 8, and from M.G.L. chapter 123, section 36B, which place greater weight on safety than on client autonomy or client confidentiality in certain, limited, situations. Sections 7 and 8, on civil commitment, state that an individual may be involuntarily placed in a psychiatric hospital when, because of a mental illness, failure to place that individual in the hospital, or discharge from the hospital, would create a likelihood of serious harm. One the three criteria for "likelihood of serious harm" is that the individual creates "a substantial risk of physical harm to other persons." Exposing another to the HIV virus could be seen as creating "a substantial risk of physical harm to other persons." Section 36B imposes upon mental health professionals a duty to protect third parties when "the patient has communicated to the licensed mental health professional an explicit threat to kill or inflict serious bodily injury upon a reasonably identified victim . . . and the patient has the apparent intent and ability to carry out that threat."

The complication is that while mandatory reporting statutes protect the mental health professional—the statutes themselves insulate the mental health professional from any legal consequences of filing a report—no such protection is attendant upon disclosing that your client is HIV positive. You therefore must take steps to insulate yourself from untoward legal consequences if you intend to disclose a client's HIV status. The law gives you the opportunity to do so insofar as numerous statutes—though none explicitly on point—favor safety over confidentiality.

If you are faced with this problem, it is probably not enough that your client is HIV positive and sexually active. You would need more to justify a decision to break confidentiality. Consider the following scenarios. An HIV positive client becomes manic and begins to have sex with numerous, anonymous partners. In this case, your client's mental illness is affecting her judgment in such a way that her capacity to protect others is impaired. That is to say, your client is placing others at significant risk because of impaired judgment, not because she has made a choice to engage in behavior that places others at risk. Another client has just discovered that he is HIV positive, and nevertheless continues to have unprotected sex with his wife of two years, *who has reason to believe that his HIV status is negative.* Each of these cases differs from the individual who knows he is HIV positive and who chooses to have unprotected sex with unwitting partners; the first, because the ego functions which allow for planning, organization, and reality testing are impaired, the second, because his partner has a reasonable belief that he is HIV negative. In instances such as these, there will be a strong argument that confidentiality may be broken and that your client's HIV status may be shared.

The disclosure of HIV status, as with all other disclosures, should follow the Law of No Surprises, the Parsimony Principle, and your profession's code of ethics. Attempt to persuade your client voluntarily to take steps to protect others, perhaps by entering a hospital on a voluntary basis, or by sharing HIV status with a partner. These alternatives would minimize the necessity of your disclosing any confidential information. If these attempts fail, and some disclosure is inevitable, disclose only that information necessary to accomplish your goal, which is to protect others at risk. Be sure to get, and document, a consultation. Even though no statute explicitly protects you from liability, the clear policy behind a series of statutes—that confidentiality yields to safety—will serve as a strong foundation for any claim against you.

13

CHILDREN AND FAMILIES

Perhaps no area of mental health law generates more intense feelings than that of children and families. Clinicians will not find this surprising: The bonds that tie children to their parents, parents to their children, and partners and siblings to one another are the strongest that humans experience. When the state intrudes into the life of a family— for however good a reason—that intensity can be felt by all involved. The questions below address circumstances in which family life is touched by the law.

QUESTIONS DISCUSSED IN THIS CHAPTER

132. Up to what age can a parent place a child in a psychiatric hospital against the child's wishes?
133. What happens when a treater recommends that a child be hospitalized, and the parents refuse to follow the recommendation?
134. Is a treater able to "pink paper" a child, or is a 51A the only means of getting a child into the hospital when the parents do not agree to a hospitalization?
135. Can a minor consent to treatment?
136. Can a minor consent to an abortion?

137. What may happen to a treater if a minor says he is 18, but after several sessions the treater discovers he is not?
138. What are the rules of confidentiality that govern the treatment of minors?
139. What's the difference between a 51A and a C and P order?
140. What's the difference between a C and P order and a CHINS?
141. What is the standard by which parental rights are terminated following a C and P order?
142. What happens if a noncustodial parent wishes to have a child treated?
143. Can a parent who has *not* been awarded legal custody of a child obtain school or medical records?
144. How does a court decide on custody when the parents can't agree?
145. In determining a custody arrangement, to what extent will a judge take a child's wishes into account?
146. Is sexual orientation a factor in adoption and custody determinations?
147. Is domestic violence taken into consideration in custody determinations?
148. What is done in Massachusetts courtrooms to make testifying against an alleged perpetrator of sexual abuse easier for a child?
149. In cases involving sexual abuse, might a therapist ever be called to testify in court about what a child has said?
150. Does Massachusetts recognize common law marriages?

DISCUSSION

132. Up to what age can a parent place a child in a psychiatric hospital against the child's wishes?

The critical age is 16. If a child is 15 years or younger, a parent may sign the child into a psychiatric hospital under a conditional voluntary, provided only that the child is "in need of care and treatment." The child will be discharged when the parents, or the hospital superintendent working with the parents, decide he is ready for discharge. If the child is 16 or 17, 104 CMR 27.10 says that he "shall have the same rights pertaining to release, withdrawal, and discharge" as do competent adult patients. For individuals 16 and over, chapter 123, sections 7 and 8 are therefore relevant: Involuntary hospitalization is an option only when failing to hospitalize would create a likelihood of serious harm (see question 23).

One slight twist: Parents may sign a child *into* the hospital against his will even if the child is 16 or 17. Signing a 16- or 17-year-old into the hospital avoids a pink paper, and the necessity of someone (such as the police) coming to the house.

133. What happens when a treater recommends that a child be hospitalized, and the parents refuse to follow the recommendation?

The treater would first review the reasons behind her recommendation, preferably with a consultant, to ensure that failure to hospitalize the minor would create a likelihood of serious harm. If, following the review, the treater still believed that a hospitalization was indicated, she would attempt to persuade the parents that a hospitalization was in their child's best interests. If the parents continued in their refusal, the treater would determine whether she had an obligation to report the situation to the Department of Social Services, pursuant to section 51A of chapter 119 (see chapter 3). If a psychiatric hospitalization were clinically indicated, it would be highly likely that the health, safety, or well-being of the child would be at stake. A report would therefore be mandated under section 51A, and at that point DSS would step in to assess the situation.

134. Is a treater able to "pink paper" a child, or is a 51A the only means of getting a child into the hospital when the parents do not agree to a hospitalization?

There is no age limit for using a pink paper (see question 31) to hospitalize an individual for 10 days. If a treater feels that a child meets commitment criteria, the treater should use a section 12 to do so. The parents may disagree and threaten to sue, but the balance should weigh heavily in favor of taking whatever steps necessary to keep the child safe, even if the steps include placing the child in a hospital by way of a pink paper.

135. Can a minor consent to treatment?

By definition, minors are not able to consent to treatment. The reason is that our society has made a judgment call: Individuals under the age of 18 cannot adequately appreciate the consequences of certain decisions. And so we say that, until the age of 18, other individuals charged with their care—such as parents—will make treatment choices on their behalf. Much as with confidentiality, the law takes this general rule and asks when exceptions are indicated. Exceptions arise in an emergency, where a situation demands immediate attention; when we have reason to believe that a minor is particularly mature, and so capable of appreciating the consequences of what she does; and when requiring parental consent would discourage the minor from receiving necessary care and treatment.

Chapter 112, section 12F addresses all three situations. First, section 12F states that "emergency examination and treatment" for a minor may proceed without consent "when delay in treatment will endanger the life, limb, or mental well-being of the patient."

Second, section 12F lists five conditions under which a minor may consent to treatment. In each of these five conditions there is reason to believe that the minor is especially mature, and so capable of making decisions without the assistance of an adult. These five are: (1) when the minor is married, widowed, or divorced; (2) when the minor is a parent; (3) when the minor is a member of the armed forces; (4) when the minor is pregnant or believes she is pregnant; (5) when the minor is living apart from her parent or guardian and is managing her own affairs.

Finally, minors may consent to treatment in circumstances where requiring parental consent would discourage the minor from receiving necessary care and treatment. Chapter 112, section12F says that a minor may consent to treatment for venereal disease. In addition, chapter 112, section 12E says that any child 12 years or older may consent to treatment for drug dependence.

See how the law balances opposing values. While minors are generally deemed not competent to consent to treatment, certain minors are especially mature. When we have reason to believe that a minor is mature, for example, because she lives apart from her parents and makes her own financial decisions, we allow that minor to make medical decisions on her own. Also, despite the presumption that minors are not competent to make treatment decisions, minors are likely *not* to tell parents about drug use and sexually transmitted diseases, and so may not get treatment if their parents must know. Because the law wants to encourage minors to get treatment, the law creates a second exception to the general rule.

Our recommendation is that, whenever possible, treaters should attempt to consult with, and obtain consent from, parents or guardians. When a minor falls into one of the five categories listed in section12F, or wishes to discuss drug use or sexually transmitted diseases, and refuses to allow you to contact the adults, then you may go ahead and begin treatment. Otherwise, it's best to treat with the blessing, or at least the knowledge, of a parent or guardian.

136. Can a minor consent to an abortion?

Chapter 112, section 12S states how an unmarried minor may obtain an abortion. The minor may either seek the consent of her parents (one parent, if the other is unavailable or does not have custody of the minor) or she may ask a judge of the superior court for approval, in which case the abortion may be performed without parental consent (or even knowledge). The judge will base her approval on whether the minor is mature enough to make the decision on her own; if the judge finds she is, the judge will authorize the physician to perform the abortion. If the judge deems the minor not sufficiently mature to make this decision, the judge will then decide whether the abortion is in the minor's best interests. If the judge deems the abortion to be in the minor's best interests, the judge will authorize the physician to perform the abortion. Such proceedings in the superior court are confidential.

137. What may happen to a treater if a minor says he is 18, but after several sessions the treater discovers he is not?

Chapter 112, section 12F protects a treater who:

> (i) relied in good faith upon the representations of such minor that he is legally able to consent to such treatment . . . or (ii) relied in good faith upon the representations of such minor that he is over eighteen years of age.

If you rely in good faith on a minor's word that he is 18 or over, or that he meets one of the criteria allowing minors to consent to treatment (see question 135), you are released from both civil and criminal liability—you can't get in trouble. But be careful: "Good faith" means making a *reasonable* effort to confirm an individual's age. If your patient says he is 18, but looks 15, you cannot simply rely on what he tells you. Make it your standard practice to ask for confirming documentation, such as a school record or driver's license, whenever you have questions about age. Be sure to document that you have done so.

138. What are the rules of confidentiality that govern the treatment of minors?

The rules of confidentiality that govern the treatment of minors are the same as the rules that govern the treatment of adults: Treaters are bound by confidentiality and testimonial privilege. Information about a minor's treatment may be shared with the minor's parent or guardian, who has legal responsibility for the child, but with no one else. The exception to sharing information with a minor's parent or guardian arises when the minor herself is able to consent to treatment (see question 135). When a minor is able to consent to treatment, chapter 112, section 12F provides that all information is confidential between the minor and the treater.

We again see how the law balances competing interests: Minors are generally not allowed to consent to treatment, so that the minor's parent or guardian, who has the authority to give consent, has access to all aspects of the minor's medical condition and treatment needs. When we deem a minor able to consent to treatment, however, it is no longer necessary for an adult to have this information, since the minor herself will be making treatment decisions. As we treat the minor like an adult in allowing her to give consent, so we treat her like an adult in making information confidential between her and her treater.

Three notes. First, even when minors are deemed able to give consent, treaters must notify parents of medical conditions so serious that "life or limb is endangered" (see chapter 112, section 12F). Second, when parents are involved in a custody dispute, such as a divorce, one parent may want to use the treatment records in the legal proceedings. The records may not be released, however, unless both parents consent. (For two possible exceptions to this rule, see the discussion of the testimonial privilege statutes in chapter 3). Finally, it may happen that a parent or guardian will ask for records, and you believe that releasing the records would not be in the minor's best interests. Perhaps, for example, an adolescent has been sexually active, or has used drugs, and your clinical judgment is that a parent or guardian ought not to have access to this information. In this case, you may refuse to release records, which will then force the parent or guardian to subpoena them. Your refusal will be buttressed if the material concerns an exception found in chapter 112, section 12F or section 12E; the argument will be that the minor has a statutory right to consent to this aspect of the treatment which, in turn, means your records covering this material are confidential. At the very least, your refusal will allow you to argue before a judge that releasing certain information would not be in your patient's best interests, and so ought not to be done.

139. What's the difference between a 51A and a C and P order?

A 51A refers to a report made under chapter 119, section 51A, the mandatory reporting statute for children (see chapter 3). A 51A is therefore a disclosure of information to the Department of Social Services that relates to the abuse or neglect of a child. A C and P order—the initials stand for "care" and "protection"—refers to a court order that removes a child from one caretaker in order to place the child in the custody of the Department of Social Services, or some other appropriate agency or individual. Chapter 119, section 24, says that any individual may petition a court to issue a C and P order. The four grounds for granting the C and P order are: (1) that the child is without "necessary" care; (2) that the child is growing up "under conditions damaging to the child's sound character development"; (3) that the child lacks proper attention; and (4) that the child's caretakers are "unwilling, incompetent, or unavailable" to care for the child.

Note that a 51A could certainly lead to a C and P order, based on what the DSS investigation reveals. The two, however, are not the same. A 51A is a disclosure of information. A C and P order places the child in the custody of another caretaker. Any individual mandated to report must file a 51A. Only a judge will author a C and P order.

140. What's the difference between a C and P order and a CHINS?

A C and P order places a child in the custody of the Department of Social Services, or some other appropriate agency or individual (see question 139). A CHINS refers to a child in need of services. As defined by chapter 119, section 21, a child in need of services is a child 16 years or younger who persistently: (1) fails to attend school; (2) violates the school's rules; (3) runs away from home; or (4) refuses to obey his parents or guardians, who are therefore rendered unable to care for him. While any individual may petition for a judge to grant a C and P order, chapter 119, section 39E states that only a parent, guardian of a child, police officer, or "supervisor of attendance" may go before a court and claim that a child meets the criteria for a CHINS. If the court determines that the child is in need of services, chapter 119, section 39G makes a number of dispositions available to the court. Possible dispositions range from therapy to placement in the custody of the Department of Social Services. Often the child is assigned a probation officer.

141. What is the standard by which parental rights are terminated following a C and P order?

In *Custody of Eleanor*, 414 Mass. 795 (1993), the SJC held that a judge must make "specific and detailed" findings in a custody proceeding, and that these findings must demonstrate parental unfitness by clear and convincing evidence. (See question 4 for a discussion of the "clear and convincing" standardof proof.)

142. What happens if a noncustodial parent wishes to have a child treated?

If the situation is an emergency, no consent is necessary. You may go ahead and treat the child, regardless of who brought her to you.

If the situation is not an emergency, you must distinguish between "legal custody" and "physical custody," terms defined by M.G.L. chapter 208, section 31. Physical custody refers to living arrangements. Physical custody does not speak to a parent's *legal* rights and responsibilities, which are determined by an award of *legal* custody to one or both parents. M.G.L. chapter 208, section31 defines "legal custody" as the legal disposition of a parent having "the right and responsibility to make major decisions regarding the child's welfare including matters of education, medical care and emotional, moral and religious development."

Only a parent with legal custody may consent to a child's treatment. That said, there is no duty to inquire about custody when a parent brings a child to you, and no requirement that you obtain the consent of both parents before you begin to treat. If, however, you are given reason to believe that the parent who has brought the child to you does not have legal custody, you must clarify the situation.

Clarification is important. If a clinician has reason to believe that the parent with legal custody has not consented to treatment, yet the clinician nevertheless proceeds to treat the child, the clinician treats *without legal consent.* If you are a physician, treating a child without consent may constitute battery, because you are touching the child without permission. Treating a child without consent may also constitute malpractice. And if anything untoward happens in the treatment, you have no defense—you shouldn't have been treating the child in the first place. So when in doubt, clarify.

143. Can a parent who has *not* been awarded legal custody of a child obtain school or medical records?

Chapter 208, section 31 states that an order granting custody "shall not negate or impede the ability of the noncustodial parent to have access to the academic, medical, hospital or other health records of the child." Parents who are not granted legal custody may obtain their child's school and medical records.

144. How does a court decide on custody when the parents can't agree?

In the Commonwealth of Massachusetts, there is no preordained set of factors a judge must consider when determining how to award custody. Really, there's very little guidance at all. The relevant statute, M.G.L. chapter 208, section 31, titled "Custody of Children," states:

> In making an order or judgment relative to the custody of children . . . the happiness and welfare of the children shall determine their custody. When considering the happiness and welfare of the child, the court shall consider whether or not the child's present or past living conditions adversely affect his physical, mental, moral, or emotional health.

The court has great latitude in determining what factors should be taken into consideration when deciding where the child's best interests lie, as the Appellate Court stated in *R.H. v. B.F.*, 39 Mass. App. Ct. 29 (1996):

> [M.G.L.] c.208, §31 [does not] specify or enumerate factors which must or should be considered in determining custody. . . . Instead, custody orders and judgments are made on the basis of a determination of the best interests of the child, and the statutes leave it to the trial judge to identify and weigh any factors found pertinent to those interests in the circumstances of the specific dispute. (39–40; footnote omitted)

The trial judge decides what factors speak to the child's best interests, and how those factors are to be weighed against one another in determining custody.

One final note—in Massachusetts, there is a presumption in favor of shared legal custody.

145. In determining a custody arrangement, to what extent will a judge take a child's wishes into account?

The rule of thumb follows common sense—as the child gets older, her preferences matter more. In *Custody of a Minor*, 383 Mass. 595 (1981), the SJC stated:

> In situations involving younger children who are not yet sufficiently mature to comprehend where their welfare lies, the courts are empowered, indeed obligated, to substitute their judgment for that of the child. (602)

In *Bak v. Bak*, 24 Mass. App. Ct. 608 (1987), and *Custody of Vaughn*, 422 Mass. 590 (1996), the Appeals Court and the SJC stated that the preference of a 10- or 11-year-old is "not given decisive weight, although it is a factor to be considered" (*Bak* at 617, *Vaughn* at 599). In *Hale v. Hale*, 12 Mass. App. Ct. 812 (1981), the Appeals Court stated that the preferences of children 9 and 13 "must be treated with caution" (820). By the time a child reaches 15, however, preference about custody arrangements may be accorded "great weight" (*Minor* at 601). Thus, the balance tips as age increases. At an early age, the judge is obligated to determine what is best for the child, regardless of preference. By the time a child reaches 15, while not necessarily decisive, her preference will matter a great deal.

146. Is sexual orientation a factor in adoption and custody determinations?

In *Adoption of Tammy*, 416 Mass. 205 (1993), the SJC held that a lesbian couple could adopt a young girl. The Court found that allowing the adoption would further "the legislative intent to promote the best interests of the child" (212). The Court's thinking was clearly based on an overwhelming consensus on the part of family, friends, and mental health professionals that the partners, Helen and Susan, were extraordinary individuals who had done a superlative job of raising Tammy. Nonetheless, the Court was clear that sexual orientation was not a bar to the adoption. It is interesting that the one judge who dissented did not disagree about whether sexual orientation should be a factor in the Court's decision. To the contrary, the dissenting judge stated explicitly, "There is nothing based on sexual orientation in the [adoption] statute which would prohibit a homosexual from . . . adopting the child" (219).

In *Bezio v. Patenaude*, 381 Mass. 563 (1980), the SJC addressed the issue of whether sexual orientation affects custody. In examining whether to award a natural mother custody of her children, the Court reasoned, "A finding that a parent is unfit to further the welfare of the child must be predicated upon parental behavior that adversely affects the child" (579). The Court then said, "In the total absence of evidence suggesting a correlation between the mother's homosexuality and her fitness as a parent, we believe the [lower court's] finding that a lesbian household would adversely affect the children to be without basis in the record" (579). The SJC's reasoning in *Bezio* strongly suggests that homosexuality, in and of itself, is not relevant to a custody determination.

147. Is domestic violence taken into consideration in custody determinations?

Custody of Vaughn, 422 Mass. 590 (1996), addresses how courts are to assess the role of domestic violence in custody disputes. In *Vaughn*, the SJC spoke with approval about a 1989 study of gender bias in the Massachusetts Court system. According to the 1989 study:

> The legislature and/or appellate courts should make it clear that abuse of any family member affects other family members and must be considered in determining the best interests of the child in connection with any order concerning custody.

The Court combined the 1989 study's conclusions with language from M.G.L. chapter 208, section 31, "In determining whether temporary shared legal custody would not be in the best interests of the child, the court shall consider . . . whether any member of the family has been the perpetrator of domestic violence." The Court then spoke eloquently about the importance of courts dealing with domestic violence in a forthright manner:

> Domestic violence is an issue too fundamental and frequently recurring to be dealt with only by implication. The very frequency of domestic violence in disputes about child custody may have the effect of inuring courts to it and thus minimizing its significance. Requiring the courts to make explicit findings about the effect of the violence on the child and the appropriateness of the custody award in light of that effect will serve to keep these matters well in the foreground of judges' thinking. (*Vaughn*, at 600)

The Court held that in custody disputes where there is a history of domestic violence, "written findings should . . . be made attending specifically to the effects of domestic violence on the child and the appropriateness of the joint custody award in light of those effects (*Vaughn* at 600, quoting *R.H. v. B.F.*, 39 Mass. App. Ct. 29, at 41 [1995]).

If the court makes an award of shared legal or physical custody, and there has been a history of domestic violence, the court must make written findings about the effects of the domestic violence on the children. The court must also explain why shared custody is appropriate in light of those effects.

148. What is done in Massachusetts courtrooms to make testifying against an alleged perpetrator of sexual abuse easier for a child?

M.G.L. chapter 278, section 16D was designed to make testifying in court easier for child witnesses. The challenge to section 16D, as to any statute that attempts to make testifying less stressful, burdensome, or traumatic, is that certain clauses of the Constitution provide criminal defendants with basic rights at trial. In the case of child witnesses in the Commonwealth, the relevant provision is found in article 12 of the Massachusetts Constitution, which states, "[E]very subject shall have a right . . . to meet the witness against him face to face." Article 12 provides the boundary of what accommodations may be made to child witnesses.

Section 16D stated that the court could offer any witness under the age of 15 an alternative to testifying on the witness stand in front of the jury and the defendant. Section 16D said that, to offer an alternative to testifying in the normal manner, the judge should hold a hearing. If, at the hearing, the judge finds by a preponderance of evidence (more likely than not; see question 4), that the child is likely "to suffer psychological or emotional trauma" in virtue of testifying either in open court or in the presence of the defendant, the child's testimony may be taken in one of two ways. One way would be to videotape the child's testimony and show it later in court. The other way would be to transmit the child's live testimony into the court, such as by closed-circuit television.

In *Commonwealth v. Bergstrom*, 402 Mass. 534 (1988), the SJC did a careful review of section 16D. The Court examined that aspect of section 16D that allowed the child to testify *outside* the presence of the defendant:

> Constitutional language more definitively guaranteeing the right to a direct confrontation between witness and accused is difficult to imagine. The plain meaning of assuring the defendant the right "*to meet* the witnesses against him *face to face*" is that the accused shall not be tried without the presence, in a court of law, of both himself and the witnesses testifying against him. To interpret the words of this mandate as requiring only that the defendant be able to see and hear the witness [on a TV monitor] renders superfluous the words "to meet" and "face to face." (542, italics in original)*

---

* In *Coy v. Iowa*, 487 U.S. 1012 (1988), the United States Supreme Court said the following about a defendant's right to confront his accuser:

> That face-to-face presence may, unfortunately, upset the truthful rape victim or abused child; but by the same token it may confound and undo the false accuser, or reveal the child coached by a malevolent adult. *It is a truism that constitutional protections have costs* [italics added]. (1020)

The Court concluded that article 12 of the Massachusetts Constitution required the child to testify *in the presence of the defendant*. That aspect of the statute providing otherwise was struck down as unconstitutional.

Second, the SJC stated that other provisions of the statute, such as testifying outside the presence of the jury, were not necessarily unconstitutional, yet were highly "suspect." The Court reasoned that there must be a "compelling need" for such an alternative to the normal manner of doing things, and that such "compelling need" would have to be shown by proof beyond a reasonable doubt:

> Such a compelling need could be shown where, by proof beyond a reasonable doubt, the recording of the testimony of a child witness outside the courtroom (but in the presence of the defendant) is shown to be necessary so as to avoid severe and long lasting emotional trauma to the child. (*Bergstrom* at 550–551)

The SJC demanded the highest standard of proof—beyond a reasonable doubt—to show that testifying outside the presence of the jury is necessary to avoid "severe and long lasting emotional trauma" to the child witness.

Third, the SJC offered ways of protecting the child witness that would not violate the Massachusetts Constitution:

> Both before and during trial, measures can be taken to reduce the adverse impact of giving testimony. By way of example, a judge may require that the environment in which a witness is to give testimony be made less formal and intimidating, and that, before and after testimony is given, appropriate court-supervised counselling [*sic*] service be made available to a witness demonstrably in need of such help. Further, consistent with the guidelines indicated here, electronically preserved testimony in the absence of the jury . . . should be allowed. These options are not exhaustive. (*Bergstrom* at 553–554)*

---

* In *Commonwealth v. Amirault*, 424 Mass. 618 (1997), the SJC elaborated upon ways a trial court could both protect a child and remain within the bounds of the Constitution:

> There is, of course, no reason why special arrangements encompassing more intimate, less intimidating settings for the child's testimony may not be devised: the number of persons present may be limited, the judge may sit at the same level as the other participants and not wear robes, special furniture may be used such as child-sized chairs and tables, the child's parent or a favorite toy may be placed near the witness. (635)

The SJC thus balanced the goals of section 16D, that of protecting child witnesses from the stress of testifying in public and in front of an alleged perpetrator, against the Massachusetts Constitution. The Constitution wins, as it will whenever a statute is inconsistent with any of its provisions. The SJC declared those aspects of the statute that were irreconcilably in conflict with article 12 void. The first conclusion: Children must testify in the presence of the defendant. The SJC then said that another part of the statute, which provided for the child to testify outside the presence of the jury, did not directly conflict with the Constitution, but was nevertheless "suspect." Judges should abide by this provision only when they absolutely must to avoid "severe and long lasting emotional trauma to the child." Finally, the SJC offered other ways of protecting children when they must testify. The history of section 16D is an excellent example of the SJC fashioning a statute with worthwhile and important goals into a shape that fits the requirements of the Massachusetts Constitution.

149. In cases involving sexual abuse, might a therapist ever be called to testify in court about what a child has said?

Yes. M.G.L. chapter 233, sections 81 and 82 set forth conditions under which someone who hears a child talk about a "sexual contact" may testify in civil and criminal proceedings about what the child said. The conditions in sections 81 and 82 are stringent, and require the court to make three findings. First, the child's out-of-court statement must be the best evidence available; if any other evidence can be found more to the point, the child's statement cannot be introduced.

Second, the child must be unavailable as a witness. The court may deem the child unavailable if the child dies; is physically or mentally ill; testifies that she cannot remember what happened; is not competent to testify, perhaps because she cannot tell the difference between a truth and a lie; or, based on a clinical examination, would suffer "severe psychological or emotional trauma" were she to testify. These conditions are captured by saying that a child is "unavailable" when she physically cannot be present in court, is not mature enough to testify about what happened, or would be severely harmed emotionally or psychologically were she to testify.

Third, the child's out-of-court statement must be "reliable." The court will find the child's statement reliable either when the child made the statement under oath, with the opportunity for cross examination, or when the judge finds that the child's statement was made "under circumstances inherently demonstrating a special guarantee of reliability." In the latter case, the judge will examine "the child's sincerity and ability to appreciate the consequences of such statement," as well as expert testimony regarding "the child's capacity to observe, remember, and give expression" to what she "has seen, heard, or experienced." Thus, the judge will examine both the child's capacity to make a reliable statement, as well as the circumstances surrounding the statement itself, in deciding whether the statement will be admitted into evidence.

If a judge finds that the child's out-of-court statement is the best evidence available, that the child is unavailable as a witness, and that the statement is reliable, the statement may be introduced at trial. If the child made the statement to a therapist, the therapist may be called upon to testify in court about what the child said.*

150. Does Massachusetts recognize common law marriages?

The Commonwealth does not recognize common law marriages, as the SJC stated without ambiguity in *Davis v. Misiano*, 373 Mass. 261 (1977), "Cohabitation within this Commonwealth, in the absence of a formal solemnization of marriage, does not create the relationship of husband and wife" (262). The *Davis* case involved a couple, Gale Davis and Louis Misiano, who had lived together and had a child. Ms. Davis asked support for herself when her relationship with Mr. Misiano ended. The SJC held that "without the existence of a marriage relation, a woman has no right to receive support." Referring to Gale Davis as "unmarried," the Court did hold Mr. Misiano responsible for "the expenses of pregnancy and confinement, as well as continuing child support" (264), but was equally clear that he was not responsible for supporting Ms. Davis.

* In *Commonwealth v. Amirault*, 424 Mass. 618 (1997), the SJC asked how M.G.L. c.233, §81 could be constitutional in light of a defendant's right to confront his accuser "face-to-face." The SJC noted that it would be impossible to confront an accuser "face-to-face" if, at trial, the therapist quotes the child—so that the child never takes the witness stand at all. The SJC nevertheless said that the mere presence of this discrepancy would not be sufficient to strike §81 down as unconstitutional. The SJC gave two reasons for its thinking: First, §81 requires that the child be "unavailable" to testify, so that someone quoting the child would be the *only* way for the evidence to be admitted at trial; second, the impact of the testimony would be much less if, instead of the child herself testifying, another person is merely quoting the child. For these two reasons, the SJC suggested in *Amirault* that §81 was not "facially unconstitutional."

AFTERWORD

The *Essentials of Massachusetts Mental Health Law* has two important points. If we've made them, we'll consider our book a success. First, laws are not made in a vacuum. Behind each law there is a value or principle the law seeks to advance. Sometimes the value is straightforward. Communications between a patient and her therapist are confidential because we want to promote the mental health of our citizenry and because we respect an individual's right to decide with whom she will share sensitive and perhaps intimate information about her life. At other times the law must balance important goals against one another. While confidentiality is important, confidentiality yields to matters of public safety. When you read a statute, regulation, or case, try to see what value the law seeks to promote or which values the law is balancing against one another. The law will make infinite more sense if you are able to find the spirit behind its letter.

The second point follows from the first: When faced with a dilemma that has legal implications, the process by which you decide becomes as important as the decision itself. Don't begin by asking, "What specific statute or regulation do I need to follow?" Begin by asking, "What's at stake here? What values are at issue, and how can I act consistent with those values?" When uncertain, seek a consultation, and carefully consider the consultant's recommendations. The process you bring to bear on your decision-making will be your greatest protection against legal troubles.

Appendix A

MASSACHUSETTS STATUTES AND REGULATIONS GOVERNING CONFIDENTIALITY, TESTIMONIAL PRIVILEGE, AND MANDATORY REPORTING

CONFIDENTIALITY: STATUTES

1. PSYCHOLOGISTS
M.G.L. c.112, §129A

All communications between a licensed psychologist and the individuals with whom the psychologist engages in the practice of psychology are confidential. At the initiation of the professional relationship the psychologist shall inform the patient of the following limitations to the confidentiality of their communications. No psychologist, colleague, agent or employee of any psychologist, whether professional, clerical, academic or therapeutic, shall disclose any information acquired or revealed in the course of or in connection with the performance of the psychologist's professional services, including the fact, circumstances, findings or records of such services, except under the following circumstances: (a) pursuant to the provisions of [the testimonial privilege statute] or any other law; (b) upon express, written consent of the patient; (c) upon the need to disclose information which protects the rights and safety of others if:

(1) the patient presents a clear and present danger to himself and refuses explicitly or by his behavior to voluntarily accept further appropriate treatment. In such circumstances, where the psychologist has a reasonable basis to believe that a patient can be committed to a hospital pursuant to chapter one hundred and twenty-three, he shall have a duty to seek said commitment. The psychologist may also contact members of the patient's family or other individuals if in the psychologist's opinion, it would assist in protecting the safety of the patient; or

(2) the patient has communicated to the psychologist an explicit threat to kill or inflict serious bodily injury upon a reasonably identified person and the patient has the apparent intent and ability to carry out the threat. In such circumstances the psychologist shall have a duty to take reasonable precautions. A psychologist shall be deemed to have taken reasonable precautions if said psychologist makes reasonable efforts to take one or more of the following actions:

(a) communicates a threat of death or serious bodily injury to a reasonably identified person;

(b) notifies an appropriate law enforcement agency in the vicinity where the patient or any potential victim resides;

(c) arranges for the patient to be hospitalized voluntarily;

(d) takes appropriate steps to initiate proceedings for involuntary hospitalization pursuant to law.

(3) the patient has a history of physical violence which is known to the psychologist and the psychologist has a reasonable basis to believe that there is a clear and present danger that the patient will attempt to kill or inflict serious bodily injury upon a reasonably identified person. In such circumstances the psychologist shall have a duty to take reasonable precautions. A psychologist shall be deemed to have taken reasonable precautions if said psychologist makes reasonable efforts to take one or more of the following actions:

(a) communicates a threat of death or serious bodily injury to a reasonably identified person;

(b) notifies an appropriate law enforcement agency in the vicinity where the patient or any potential victim resides;

(c) arranges for the patient to be hospitalized voluntarily;

(d) takes appropriate steps to initiate proceedings for involuntary hospitalization pursuant to law.

(4) nothing contained herein shall require a psychologist to take any action which, in the exercise of reasonable professional judgment, would endanger himself or increase the danger to a potential victim or victims.

(5) the psychologist shall only disclose that information which is essential in order to protect the rights and safety of others.

(d)* in order to collect amounts owed by the patient for professional services rendered by the psychologist or his employees; provided, however, that the psychologist may only disclose the nature of services provided, the dates of services, the amount due for services and other relevant financial information; provided, further, that if the patient raises as a defense to said action substantive assertions concerning the competence of the psychologist or the quality of the services provided, the psychologist may disclose whatever information is necessary to rebut such assertions; or

(e) in such other situations as shall be defined in the rules and regulations of the board.

No provision of this section shall be construed to prevent a nonprofit hospital service or medical service corporation from inspecting and copying, in the ordinary course of determining eligibility for or entitlement to benefits, any and all records relating to diagnosis, treatment, or other services provided to any person, including a minor or incompetent, for which coverage, benefit or reimbursement is claimed, so long as the policy or certificate under which the claim is made provides that such access to such records is permitted.

2. SOCIAL WORKERS
M.G.L. c.112, §135A

All communications between a social worker licensed pursuant to the provisions of section one hundred and thirty-two or a social worker employed in a state, county, or municipal governmental agency, and a client are confidential. During the initial phase of the professional relationship, such social worker shall inform the client of such confidential communications and the limitations thereto as set forth in this section

* (a), (b), (c) do not exist in the original.

and [the testimonial privilege statute], in accordance with sound professional practice.

No such social worker, colleague, agent or employee of any social worker, whether professional, clerical, academic or therapeutic, shall disclose any information acquired or revealed in the course of or in connection with the performance of the social worker's professional services, including the fact, circumstances, findings or records of such services, except under the following circumstances:

(a) pursuant to the provisions of this section and [the testimonial privilege statute] or any other law.

(b) upon express, written consent of such client or, in the event of a client incompetent to consent, or a guardian appointed to act in the client's behalf;

(c) upon the need to disclose that information which is necessary to protect the safety of the client or others if

(1) the client presents a clear and present danger to himself and refuses explicitly to voluntarily accept further appropriate treatment. In such circumstances, where the social worker has a reasonable basis to believe that a client can be committed to a hospital pursuant to section twelve of chapter one hundred and twenty-three, the social worker shall take appropriate steps within the legal scope of social work practice, to initiate proceedings for involuntary hospitalization. The social worker may also contact members of the client's family or other individuals if in the social worker's opinion, it would assist in protecting the safety of the client;

(2) the client has communicated to the social worker an explicit threat to kill or inflict serious bodily injury upon a reasonably identified victim or victims and the client has the apparent intent and ability to carry out the threat or has a history of physical violence which is known to the social worker and the social worker has a reasonable basis to believe that there is a clear and present danger that the client will attempt to kill or inflict serious bodily injury against a reasonably identified victim or victims. In either of such circumstances, any duty owed by a social worker to warn or in any other way protect a potential victim shall be discharged if the social worker takes reasonable precautions. No cause of action shall lie against, nor shall legal liability be imposed against, a social worker for failure to warn or in any other way protect a potential victim or victims, unless the social worker fails to take reasonable precautions. Nothing in this paragraph shall require a social worker to take any actions which, in the exercise of reasonable professional judgment, would en-

danger such social worker or increase the danger to a potential victim or victims;

(d)* in order to collect amounts owed by the client for professional services rendered by the social worker or his employee; provided, however, that the social worker may disclose only the nature of services provided, the dates of the services, the amount due for services and other relevant financial information; and, provided, further, that if the client raises as a defense to said action substantive assertions concerning the competence of the social worker or the quality of the services provided, the social worker may disclose whatever information is necessary to rebut such assertions;

(e)–(h) [where the social worker has initiated a proceeding or acquired information during the course of a legally mandated investigation into an abused child or an abused elderly person];

(i) in the case of marital therapy, family therapy or consultation in contemplation of therapy, with the written consent of each adult patient participant.

The provision of information acquired by a social worker from a client to any insurance company, nonprofit hospital service corporation, medical service corporation or health maintenance organization or to a board established pursuant to section twelve of chapter one hundred and twenty-six B, pertaining to the administration of provision of benefits, including utilization review or peer review, provided for expenses arising from the out-patient diagnosis or treatment or both, of mental or nervous conditions, shall not constitute a waiver or breach of any right to which said client is otherwise entitled under this section.

[Same final paragraph as in psychologist statute]

3. ALLIED MENTAL HEALTH AND HUMAN SERVICES PROFESSIONALS†
M.G.L. c.112, §172

Any communication between an allied mental health or human services professional and a client shall be deemed to be confidential. Said privi-

---

* (a), (b), (c) do not exist in the original.

† M.G.L c.112, §163 defines allied mental health and human services professionals as "a licensed marriage and family therapist, a licensed rehabilitation counselor, a licensed educational psychologist or a licensed mental health counselor."

lege shall be subject to waiver only in the following circumstances:

(a) where the allied mental health and human services professional is a party defendant to a civil, criminal or disciplinary action arising from such practice in which case the waiver shall be limited to that action;

(b) where the client is a defendant in a criminal proceeding and the use of the privilege would violate the defendant's right to compulsory process and right to present testimony and witnesses in his own behalf;

(c) when the communication reveals the contemplation or commission of a crime or a harmful act; and

(d) where a client agrees to the waiver, or in circumstances where more than one person in a family is receiving therapy, where each such family member agrees to the waiver.

The provisions of this section shall not be construed to prevent third party reimburser from inspecting and copying, in the ordinary course of determining eligibility for or entitlement to benefits, any and all records relating to diagnosis, treatment or other services provided to any person, including a minor or incompetent, for which coverage, benefit or reimbursement is claimed, so long as the policy or certificate under which the claim is made provides that such access to such records is permitted. The provisions of this section shall not be construed to prevent access to any such records pursuant to any peer review or utilization review procedures applied and implemented in good faith.

4. DEPARTMENT OF MENTAL HEALTH
M.G.L. c.123, §36

The department shall keep records of the admission, treatment and periodic review of all persons admitted to facilities under its supervision Such records shall be private and not open to public inspection except (1) upon proper judicial order whether or not in connection with pending judicial proceedings, (2) that the commissioner shall allow the attorney of a patient or resident to inspect records of said patient or resident if requested to do so by the patient, resident or attorney, and (3) that the commissioner may permit inspection or disclosure when in the best interest of the patient or resident as provided in the rules and regulations of the department. This section shall govern the patient records of the department notwithstanding any other provision of law.

5. SEXUAL ASSAULT COUNSELORS
M.G.L. c.233, §20J

As used in this section the following words, unless the context clearly requires otherwise shall have the following meaning: . . .

"Sexual assault counsellor [sic]," a person who is employed by or is a volunteer in a rape crisis center, has undergone thirty-five hours of training who reports to and is under the direct control and supervision of a licensed social worker, nurse, psychiatrist, psychologist or psychotherapist and whose primary purpose is the rendering of advice, counseling or assistance to victims of sexual assault.

"Victim," a person who has suffered a sexual assault and who consults a sexual assault counsellor [sic] for the purpose of securing advice, counseling or assistance concerning a mental, physical or emotional condition caused by such sexual assault . . ."

A sexual assault counsellor [sic] shall not disclose such confidential communication without the prior written consent of the victim; provided, however, that nothing in this chapter shall be construed to limit the defendant's right of cross-examination of such counsellor [sic] in a civil or criminal proceeding if such counsellor [sic] testifies with such written consent.

Such confidential communications shall not be subject to discovery and shall be inadmissible in any criminal or civil proceeding without the prior written consent of the victim to whom the report, record, working paper or memorandum relates.

6. DOMESTIC VIOLENCE VICTIMS' COUNSELORS
M.G.L. c.233, §20K

As used in this section, the following words shall unless the context clearly requires otherwise have the following meanings:

"Abuse," causing or attempting to cause physical harm placing another in fear of imminent physical harm; causing another to engage in sexual relations against his will by force, threat of force, or coercion. . . .

"Domestic violence victims' counselor," a person who is employed or volunteers in a domestic violence victims' program, who has undergone a minimum of twenty-five hours of training and who reports to and is under the direct control and supervision of a direct service supervisor of a domestic violence victims' program, and whose primary purpose is the rendering of advice, counseling or assistance to victims of abuse.

"Domestic violence victims' program," any refuge, shelter, office, safe home, institution or center established for the purpose of offering assistance to victims of abuse through crisis intervention, medical, legal or support counseling

"Victim," a person who suffered abuse and who consults a domestic violence victims' counselor for the purpose of securing advice, counseling or assistance concerning a mental, physical or emotional condition caused by such abuse.

A domestic violence victims' counselor shall not disclose such confidential communication without the prior written consent of the victim, except as hereinafter provided. Such confidential communication shall not be subject to discovery in any civil , legislative or administrative proceeding without the prior written consent of the victim to whom such confidential communication relates. In criminal actions such confidential communications shall be subject to discovery and shall be admissible as evidence but only to the extent of information contained therein which is exculpatory in relation to the defendant; provided, however, that the court shall first examine such confidential communication and shall determine whether or not such exculpatory information is therein contained before allowing such discovery or the introduction of such evidence.

Confidentiality: Regulations

1. **Department of Mental Health**
   104 CMR 27.18
2. **Psychologists**
   251 CMR 1.11
3. **Social Workers**
   258 CMR 22.01 and 22.02

1. DEPARTMENT OF MENTAL HEALTH
104 CMR 27.18

(6) Except as provided below, all records relating to any persons admitted to or treated by a facility shall be private and not open to public inspection except as provided in this section.

(a) Records of patients shall be open to inspection upon proper judicial order . . .

(b) The Commissioner or designee shall permit the attorney of a patient to inspect the records of said patient upon the request of the patient or attorney . . .

(c) A patient and the patient's legally authorized representative shall be permitted to inspect the patient's records absent a determination by the Commissioner or designee that inspection by the patient will result in harm to the patient . . .

(d) The Department may disclose records as required by [the Sex Offender Registry Law].

(e) The Commissioner or designee may in his or her discretion permit inspection or disclosure of records of a patient, upon the written request of a third party where the Commissioner or designee has made a determination that such inspection or disclosure would be in the best interest of the patient. Prior to authorizing any release of records under this section, other than by court order or to the attorney for a patient, the Commissioner or designee shall, whenever possible, seek the informed written consent of the patient, . . . or the patient's legally authorized representative.

(f) Without limiting the discretionary authority of the Commissioner or designee to identify other situations where inspection or disclosure is in the patient's best interest, such inspection or disclosure may be made in the patient's best interest in the following cases:

1. to the receiving facility, when the patient meets the criteria for commitment . . . and transfer to that facility is being requested.

2. to a physician who requests such records for the treatment of a medical or psychiatric emergency . . .

3. when the record will enable the patient, or someone acting on his or her behalf, to pursue a claim, suit or other legal remedy, to enforce a right, or to defend himself or herself against such action.

4. to ensure that the civil rights of the patient are protected.

5. to enable the patient or resident, or someone acting on his or her behalf, to obtain third party payment for services rendered to such patient; or

4. [sic] to persons conducting an investigation [involving harm to a DMH patient

6. [sic] to persons engaged in research approved by the Department . . .

(g) Any disclosure pursuant to the exceptions outlined in 104 CMR 27.18 (6) (a)–(e) shall be limited to the record or information necessary to achieve the purpose of the exception.

2. PSYCHOLOGISTS
251 CMR 1.11

. . . all communications between a licensed psychologist and the individuals with whom the psychologist engages in the practice of psychology shall be deemed to be and treated as confidential in perpetuity.

(1) Notwithstanding the provisions of [the psychologist confidentiality statute] information which is acquired by a psychologist pursuant to the professional practice of psychology, whether directly or indirectly, may

be disclosed, without client consent, written or otherwise, to another appropriate professional as part of a professional consultation which is designed to enhance the services provided to a client or clients. In disclosing such information, psychologists shall use their best efforts to safeguard the client's privacy by not disclosing the client's name or other identifying demographic information, or any other information by which the client might be identified by the consultant, unless such information is, in the psychologist's judgment, necessary for the consultation to be successful.

(2)(a) The reference to "initiation of the professional relationship" in [the psychologist confidentiality statute] shall mean that the client must be informed of the limits on confidentiality by the end of the first professional session, unless there are documented substantial clinical reasons for withholding such information and the decision to withhold such information is reviewed and redocumented on a regular basis. Moreover, if the client has come to the psychologist specifically for psychological evaluation, court ordered evaluation, or psychological testing, the client shall be informed about all confidentiality limitations before said evaluation or testing begins.

(b) In the event that, before the psychologist has an opportunity to inform the client concerning the limits on confidentiality, a client begins to discuss matters which the psychologist knows, or in the exercise of his/her professional judgment should know, are likely to result in the psychologist's having to reveal confidential information without the client's consent, then the psychologist shall immediately inform the patient of the limits on confidentiality.

3. SOCIAL WORKERS
258 CMR 22.01 and 22.02

22.01
No person licensed [as a social worker] or an employee of such person may disclose any information he/she may have acquired from person consulting him/her in his/her professional capacity except:

(1) With the written consent of the person or, in the case of death or disability, of his/her own personal representative, of any other person authorized to sue, or of the beneficiary of an insurance policy on that

person's life, health, or physical condition;

(2) That a licensed certified social worker, including those engaged in independent clinical practice, and those practicing as licensed social workers or as licensed social work associates, shall not be required to treat as confidential a communication that reveals the contemplation or commission of a crime or harmful act;

(3) When the person waives the requirement of confidentiality by bringing charges against the licensed certified social worker, the independent clinical practitioner, the licensed social worker, or the licensed social work associate.

(4) If the licensee has reasonable grounds to suspect that a child has been abused or neglected.

(5) Communications made in the course of a social work examination ordered by a court of competent jurisdiction when the client has been informed before the examination that any communications made during the communication would not be privileged.

22.02

Nothing in this chapter shall be construed to authorize or require any conduct inco nsistent with the mandates of [the child abuse mandatory reporting statute].

Testimonial Privilege: Statutes

1. **Psychotherapists**
   M.G.L. c.233, §20B
2. **Social Workers**
   M.G.L. c.112, §135B

1. PSYCHOTHERAPISTS
M.G.L. c.233, §20B

The following words as used in this section shall have the following meanings:

"Patients," a person who, during the course of diagnosis or treatment, communicates with a psychotherapist;

"Psychotherapist," a person licensed to practice medicine, who devotes a substantial portion of his time to the practice of psychiatry. "Psychotherapist" shall also include a person who is licensed as a psychologist by the board of registration of psychologists or a person who is a registered nurse licensed by the board of registration in nursing whose certificate of registration has been endorsed authorizing the practice of professional nursing in an expanded role as a psychiatric nurse mental health clinical specialist, pursuant to the provisions of section eighty B of chapter one hundred and twelve.

"Communications" includes conversations, correspondence, actions and occurrences relating to diagnosis or treatment before, during or after institutionalization, regardless of the patient's awareness of such conversations, correspondence, actions and occurrences, and any records, memoranda or notes of the foregoing.

Except as hereinafter provided, in any court proceeding and in any proceeding preliminary thereto and in legislative and administrative proceedings, a patient shall have the privilege of refusing to disclose, and of preventing a witness from disclosing, any communication, wherever made, between said patient and a psychotherapist relative to the diagnosis or treatment of the patient's mental or emotional condition. This privilege shall apply to patients engaged with a psychotherapist in marital therapy, family therapy, or consultation in contemplation of such therapy. . . .

The privilege granted hereunder shall not apply to any of the following communications:

(a) If a psychotherapist, in the course of his diagnosis or treatment of the patient, determines that the patient is in need of treatment in a hospital for mental or emotional illness or that there is a threat of imminently dangerous activity by the patient against himself or another person, and on the basis of such determination discloses such communication either for the purpose of placing or retaining the patient in such hospital, provided, however, that the provisions of this section shall continue in effect after the patient is in said hospital, or placing the patient under arrest or under the supervision of law enforcement authorities.

(b) If a judge finds that the patient, after having been informed that the communications would not be privileged, has made the communications to a psychotherapist in the course of a psychiatric examination ordered by the court, provided that such communications shall be admissible only on issues involving the patient's mental or emotional condition but not as a confession or admission of guilt.

(c) In any proceeding, except one involving child custody, adoption or adoption consent, in which the patient introduces his mental or emotional condition as an element of his claim or defense, and the judge or presiding officer finds that it is more important to the interests of justice that the communication be disclosed than that the relationship between the patient and the psychotherapist be protected.

(d) In any proceeding after the death of a patient in which his mental or emotional condition is introduced by any party claiming or defending through or as beneficiary of the patient as an element of the claim or defense, and the judge or presiding officer finds that it is more important to the interests of justice that the communication be disclosed than that the relationship between the psychotherapist and patient be protected.

(e) In any case involving child custody, adoption or the dispensing with the need for consent to adoption in which, upon a hearing in chambers, the judge, in the exercise of his discretion, determines that the psychotherapist has evidence bearing significantly on the patient's ability to provide suitable care or custody, and that it is more important to the welfare of the child that the communication be disclosed than that the relationship between patient and psychotherapist be protected; provided, however, that in such cases of adoption or the dispensing with the need for consent to adoption, a judge shall determine that the patient has been informed that such communication would not be privileged.

(f) In any proceeding brought by the patient against the psychotherapist, and in any malpractice, criminal or license revocation proceeding, in which disclosure is necessary to the claim or defense of the psychotherapist.

2. SOCIAL WORKERS
M.G.L. c.112, §135B

Except as hereinafter provided, in any court proceeding and in any proceeding preliminary thereto and in legislative and administrative proceedings, a client shall have the privilege of refusing to disclose and of preventing a witness from disclosing any communication, wherever made, between said client and a social worker licensed pursuant to the provisions of section one hundred and thirty-two of chapter one hundred and twelve, or a social worker employed in a state, county or municipal governmental agency, relative to the diagnosis or treatment of the client's mental or emotional condition. . . .

The privilege granted hereunder shall not apply to any of the following communications:

(a) If a social worker, in the course of making a diagnosis or treating the client, determines that the client is in need of treatment in a hospital for mental or emotional illnesses or that there is a threat of imminently dangerous activity by the client against himself or another person, and on the basis of such determination discloses such communication either for the purpose of placing or retaining the client in such hospital; provided, however, that the provisions of this section shall continue in effect after the client is in said hospital, or placing the client under arrest or under the supervision of law enforcement authorities;

(b) If a judge finds that the client, after having been informed that the communications would not be privileged, has made the communications to a social worker in the course of a psychiatric examination ordered by the court; provided, however, that such communications shall be admissible only on issues involving the client's mental or emotional condition but not as a confession or admission of guilt;

(c) In any proceeding, except one involving child custody, adoption or adoption consent, in which the client introduces his mental or emotional condition as an element of his claim or defense, and the judge or presiding officer finds that it is more important to the interests of justice that the communication be disclosed than that the relationship between the client and the social worker be protected;

(d) In any proceeding after the death of a client in which his mental or emotional condition is introduced by any party claiming or defending through or as beneficiary of the client as an element of the claim or defense, and the judge or presiding officer finds that it is more important to the interests of justice that the communication be disclosed than that the relationship between the client and the social worker be protected;

(e)–(f) In the initiation of proceedings [for the protection of children, the elderly or disabled persons];

(g) In any other case involving child custody, adoption or the dispensing with the need for consent to adoption in which, upon a hearing in chambers, the judge, in the exercise of his discretion, determines that the social worker has evidence bearing significantly on the client's ability to provide suitable care or custody, and that it is more important to the welfare of the child that the communication be disclosed than that the relationship between client and social worker be protected; provided, however, that in such case of adoption or the dispensing with the need for consent to adoption, a judge shall determine that the client has been informed that such communications would not be privileged; or

(h) In any proceeding brought by the client against the social worker and in any malpractice, criminal or license revocation proceeding in which disclosure is necessary or relevant to the claim or defense of the social worker.

Mandatory Reporting

1. ELDERLY PERSONS
M.G.L. c.19A, §§14 and 15

§14

For the purposes of sections fourteen to twenty-six, inclusive, the following words and terms shall, unless the context otherwise requires, have the following meaning:

"Abuse," an act or omission which results in serious physical or emotional injury to an elderly person or financial exploitation of an elderly person . . .

"Caretaker," the person responsible for the care of an elderly person, which responsibility may arise as the result of a family relationship, or by a voluntary or contractual duty undertaken on behalf of an elderly person, or may arise by a fiduciary duty imposed by law. . . .

"Elderly person," an individual who is sixty years of age or over. . . .

"Financial exploitation," an act or omission by another person, which causes a substantial monetary or property loss to an elderly person, or causes a substantial monetary or property gain to the other person, which gain would otherwise benefit the elderly person but for the act or omission of such other person . . .

§15

(a) Any physician, physician assistant, medical intern, dentist, nurse, family counselor, probation officer, social worker, policeman, firefighter, emergency medical technician, licensed psychologist, coroner, registered physical therapist, registered occupational therapist, osteopath, podiatrist, executive director of a licensed home health agency or executive director of a homemaker service agency who has reasonable cause to believe that an elderly person is suffering from or has died as a result of abuse, shall immediately make a verbal report of such information or cause a report to be made to the department or its designated agency and shall within forty-eight hours make a written report to the department or its designated agency. Any person so required to make such reports who fails to do so shall be punished by a fine of not more than one thousand dollars. . . .

(c) In addition to a person required to report under the provisions of subsection (a) of this section, any other person may make such a report to the department or its designated agency, if any such person has reasonable cause to believe that an elderly person is suffering from or has died as a result of abuse.

(d) No person required to report pursuant to the provisions of subsection (a) shall be liable in any civil or criminal action by reason of such report; provided, however, that such person did not perpetrate, inflict or cause said abuse. No other person making such a report pursuant to the provisions of subsection (b) or (c) shall be liable in any civil or criminal action by reason of such report if it was made in good faith . . . No employer or supervisor may discharge, demote, transfer, reduce pay, benefits or work privileges, prepare a negative work performance evaluation, or take any other action detrimental to an employee or supervisee who files a report in accordance with the provisions of this section by reason of such report.

(e) Reports made pursuant to subsections (a) and (b) shall contain the name, address and approximate age of the elderly person who is the subject of the report, information regarding the nature and extent of the abuse, the name of the person's caretaker, if known, any medical treatment being received or immediately required, if known, any other information the reporter believes to be relevant to the investigation, and the name and address of the reporter and where said reporter may be contacted, if the reporter wishes to provide said information. The department shall publicize the provisions of this section and the process by which reports of abuse shall be made.

(f) [Any statute or regulation] relating to the exclusion of confidential communications shall not prohibit the filing of a report pursuant to the provisions of subsection (a), (b) or (c).

2. DISABLED PERSONS
M.G.L. c.19C, §§1, 10, and 11

§1

As used in this chapter, the following words shall, unless the context requires otherwise, have the following meanings:

"Abuse," an act or omission which results in serious physical or emotional injury to a disabled person . . .

"Disabled person," a person between the ages of eighteen to fifty-nine, inclusive, who is mentally retarded . . . or who is otherwise mentally or physically disabled and as a result of such mental or physical disability is wholly or partially dependent on others to meet his daily living needs. . . .

"Mandated reporter," any physician, medical intern, hospital personnel engaged in the examination, care or treatment of persons, medical examiner, dentist, psychologist, nurse, chiropractor, podiatrist, osteopath, public or private school teacher, educational administrator, guidance or family counselor, day care worker, probation officer, social worker, foster parent, police officer or person employed by a state agency . . . or employed by a private agency providing services to disabled persons who, in his professional capacity shall have reasonable cause to believe that a disabled person is suffering from a reportable condition.

"Reportable condition," a serious physical or emotional injury resulting from abuse, including unconsented to sexual activity.

§14

Except when prevented by the constraints of professional privilege as hereinafter provided, mandated reporters shall notify the [Disabled Persons Protection Commission] orally of any reportable condition immediately upon becoming aware of such condition and shall report in writing within forty-eight hours after such oral report. . . .

Any person may file report [sic] if such person has reasonable cause to believe that a disabled person is suffering from abuse or has died as a result thereof.

No mandated reporter shall be liable in any civil or criminal action by reason of submitting a report. No other person shall be liable in any civil or criminal action by reason of submitting a report if such report was made in good faith . . .

No privilege . . . relating to the exclusion of confidential communications and the competency of witnesses may be invoked to prevent a report by a mandated reporter or in any civil action arising out of a report made pursuant to this chapter; provided, however, that a mandated reporter need not report an otherwise reportable condition if the disabled person invokes a privilege, established by law or professional code, to maintain the confidentiality of communications with such mandated reporter.

§11
No person shall discharge or cause to be discharged or otherwise discipline or in any manner discriminate against or threaten any employee, client or other person for filing a report with the commission or testifying in any commission proceeding, or providing information to the commission . . .

3. PATIENTS AND RESIDENTS IN FACILITIES LICENSED BY THE DEPARTMENT OF PUBLIC HEALTH M.G.L. c.111, §§72F and 72G

§72F
In sections 72F to 72L, inclusive, the following words shall have the following meanings:

"Abuse," physical contact which harms or is likely to harm the patient or resident.

"Mistreatment," use of medications, isolation, or use of physical or chemical restraints which harms or is likely to harm the patient or resident.

"Neglect," the failure to provide treatment and services necessary to maintain the health and safety of the patient or resident . . .

"Facility," any facility required to be licensed [by the Department of Public Health].

§72G

Any physician, medical intern, registered nurse, licensed practical nurse, nurse's aide, orderly, medical examiner, dentist, optometrist, optician, chiropractor, podiatrist, coroner, police officer, speech pathologist, audiologist, social worker, pharmacist, physical or occupational therapist or health officer, paid for caring for a patient or resident in a facility who has reasonable cause to believe that a patient or resident of a facility has been abused, mistreated or neglected shall immediately report such abuse, mistreatment or neglect to the department by oral communication and by making a written report within forty-eight hours after such oral communication. Any such person so required to make such oral and written reports who fails to do so shall be punished by a fine of not more than one thousand dollars.

In addition to those persons required to report pursuant to this section, any other person may make such a report if any such person has reasonable cause to believe that a patient or resident of a facility has been abused, mistreated or neglected. Any person making an oral or written report pursuant to this section shall not be liable in any civil or criminal action by reason of such report if it was made in good faith.

No facility shall discharge, or in any manner discriminate or retaliate against any person who, in good faith, makes such a report, or testifies, or is about to testify in any proceeding about the abuse, mistreatment or neglect of patients or residents in said facilities. A facility which discharges, discriminates or retaliates against such a person shall be liable to the person so discharged, discriminated against or retaliated against, for treble damages, costs and attorney's fees.

Said written reports shall contain the following information: the name and sex of the patient or resident; the name and address of the facility in which he resides; the age of the patient or resident, if known to the reporter; the name and address of the reporter and where said reporter may be contacted; any information relative to the nature and extent of the abuse, mistreatment or neglect, and, if known to the reporter, any information relative to prior abuse, mistreatment or neglect of such patient or resident; the circumstances under which the reporter became aware of the abuse, mistreatment or neglect; if known to the reporter, whatever action, if any, was taken to treat or otherwise assist the patient or resident; any other information which the reporter believes might be helpful in establishing the cause of such abuse, mistreatment or neglect and the person or persons responsible therefor; and such other information as may be required by the department [of public health].

Any privilege . . . relating to the exclusion of confidential communications and the competency of witnesses, may not be invoked in any civil action arising out of a report made pursuant to this section.

4. CHILDREN
M.G.L. c.119, §51A

Any physician, medical intern, hospital personnel engaged in the examination, care or treatment of persons, medical examiner, psychologist, emergency medical technician, dentist, nurse, chiropractor, podiatrist, osteopath, public or private school teacher, educational administrator, guidance or family counselor, day care worker or any person paid to care for or work with a child in any public or private facility, or home or program funded by the commonwealth . . . which provides day care or residential services to children or which provides the services of child care resource and referral agencies, voucher management agencies, family day care systems and child care food programs, probation officer, clerk/magistrate of the district courts, parole officer, social worker, foster parent, firefighter or policeman, office for children licensor, school attendance officer, allied mental health and human services professional, drug and alcoholism counselor, psychiatrist, and clinical social worker who, in his professional capacity shall have reasonable cause to believe that a child under the age of eighteen years is suffering physical or emotional injury resulting from abuse inflicted upon him which causes harm or substantial risk of harm to the child's health or welfare including sexual abuse, or from neglect, including malnutrition, or who is determined to be physically dependent upon an addictive drug at birth, shall immediately report such condition to the department [of social services] by oral communication and by making a written report within forty-eight hours after such oral communication; provided, however, that whenever such person so required to report is a member of the staff of a medical or other public or private institution, school or facility, he shall immediately either notify the department or notify the person in charge of such institution, school or facility, or that person's designated agent, whereupon such person in charge or his said agent shall then become responsible to make the report in the manner required by this section. Any such person so required to make such oral and written reports who fails to do so shall be punished by a fine of not more than one thousand dollars. Any person who knowingly files a report of child abuse that is frivolous shall be punished by a fine of not more than one thousand dollars.

Said reports shall contain the names and addresses of the child and his parents or other person responsible for his care, if known; the child's age; the child's sex; the nature and extent of the child's injuries, abuse, maltreatment or neglect, including any evidence of prior injuries, abuse, maltreatment, or neglect; the circumstances under which the person required to report first became aware of the child's injuries, abuse, maltreatment or neglect; whatever action, if any, was taken to treat, shelter, or otherwise assist the child; the name of the person or persons making such report; and any other information which the person reporting believes might be helpful in establishing the cause of the injuries; the identity of the person or persons responsible therefor; and such other information as shall be required by the department [of social services]. . . .

In addition to those persons required to report pursuant to this section, any other person may make such a report if any such person has reasonable cause to believe that a child is suffering from or has died as a result of such abuse or neglect. No person so required to report shall be liable in any civil or criminal action by reason of such report. No other person making such report shall be liable in any civil or criminal action by reason of such report if it was made in good faith . . .

No employer of those persons required to report pursuant to this section shall discharge, or in any manner discriminate or retaliate against any person who in good faith makes such a report, testifies or is about to testify in any proceeding involving child abuse or neglect. Any such employer who discharges, discriminates or retaliates against such a person shall be liable to such person for treble damages, costs and attorney's fees.

Within sixty days of the receipt of a report by the department [of social services] from any person required to report, the department shall notify such person, in writing, of its determination of the nature, extent and cause of the injuries to the child, and the social services that the department intends to provide to the child or his family.

Any privilege established by [statute] relating to confidential communications shall not prohibit the filing of a report pursuant to the provisions of this section . . .

Appendix B

SAMPLE FORMS AND LETTERS

Subpoena
Reply to a Board of Registration Letter of Complaint
Informed Consent Letter for a Psychodynamic Psychotherapy
Letter Terminating a Therapy Relationship

SUBPOENA

On the next page is an example of a subpoena. The subpoena has a somewhat intimidating quality; most probably because it is intended to intimidate. Remember, though, that a subpoena is a demand for your <u>appearance</u>. Once you have appeared, you have fulfilled your obligation. A subpoena does not allow you to release records or to discuss confidential information, and doing either without a court order or client consent—notwithstanding that you have received a subpoena—will expose you to liability for having breached your client's confidentiality.

FORTHWITH

COMMONWEALTH OF MASSACHUSETTS
SUBPOENA DUCES TECUM

Middlesex, SS.

To: Dr. Richard Coyle:

Greetings.

You are hereby required, in the name of the Commonwealth of Massachusetts, to appear before the District Court Department, holden at Marlboro within and for the county of Middlesex on the 21 day of June, 1997, at 11 O'clock in the *forenoon,* and from day to day thereafter, until the action hereinafter named is heard by said court, to give evidence of what you know relating to an action of a juvenile matter then and there to be heard and tried between the *Commonwealth of Massachusetts,* plaintiff, and *William Hubbs,* defendant,

and

You are further required to bring with you any and all medical records for

William Hubbs Junior.

HEREOF FAIL NOT, as failure by any person without adequate excuse to obey a subpoena served upon him may be deemed contempt of court in which action is pending.

HEREOF FAIL NOT, as you will answer your default under the pains and penalties in the law in the behalf made and provided.

Dated at Danvers, Massachusetts, the 10 day of June, A.D. 1997.

_____

Notary Public
My Commission expires 4/20/99

Reply to a
Board of Registration
Letter of Complaint

Your initial response to a board of registration should be a request that the individual who made the complaint provide a release of information. Without a release, providing a substantive response—a response that discloses confidential information—could lay the basis for another claim against you, for breach of confidentiality.

Once you receive a release and are prepared respond to the complaint itself, be sure to consult with your malpractice carrier. Your response to the complaint is "discoverable," which means that if the matter goes to court, the other side's lawyer will have the opportunity to read your letter and possibly use it to your disadvantage. Also, a well-written response is likely to end the matter. For these reasons, it is wise to consult with your carrier as you draft your letter.

Ms. Curtiss
Board of Registration in Psychology
Boston, MA 02115

April 19, 1997
RE: complaint #PHD-97-1347

Dear Ms. Curtiss,

I have received your letter of April 14, 1997, that contained a complaint from Mr. Mark Foster. It is my understanding of patient-therapist confidentiality that I am required to have a consent from the patient before I may release any information concerning a treatment.* If you would forward a copy of Mr. Foster's consent giving me permission to discuss this matter with your Board, as well as to share his record with you, I will provide a response to the complaint.

I will assume that the 30-day period of time for my response will not begin to run until I have received Mr. Foster's consent to release information.

Thank you for your understanding in this matter.

Sincerely,

Dr. Saks

---

* The consent to release information should include *all* treaters involved in the patient's care. Thus, an additional paragraph might read:

I note from my records that I consulted with Dr. Wizner and Dr. Parrish during the course of Mr. Foster's treatment. Because it will be necessary for my response to include their input about Mr. Foster's treatment, I would ask that Mr. Foster also provide consents for Drs. Wizner and Parrish to release information. Mr. Foster's consent for Drs. Wizner and Parrish to release information may be sent to me directly, or to Dr. Wizner and Dr. Foster at the addresses below.

Informed Consent Letter for a Psychodynamic Psychotherapy

Following is an example of an informed consent letter; this particular letter involves a psychodynamic psychotherapy, as the second paragraph explains. Clinicians have _very_ different responses to the idea of using such a letter. While some clinicians find letters helpful in making the frame of a psychotherapy clear at the outset, other clinicians would not even consider using written material to start off a therapeutic relationship, mostly because of what they see as detrimental implications for the transference.

Most important is that at the beginning of your work, enough information is conveyed for your prospective client to make a reasoned judgment about whether to begin a therapy with you. Whether this information is conveyed in a letter, a form, or orally, is not as important as that your client understand the nature of what you do, as well as the essential elements of the frame. Note, however, that the letter contains a significant amount of information, probably more than can be absorbed in a single sitting, especially since most clients are somewhat anxious at a first session. From this perspective, a written explanation of how you work affords a client the opportunity to review what you've said in a more relaxed setting.

As this letter makes clear, important aspects of the therapy—such as what gets talked about, how often sessions are held, and how long the therapy lasts—are left to be decided as the psychotherapy progresses. In this sense, the letter does not constitute informed consent; rather, it *informs the client about nonnegotiable aspects of your work, and encourages discussion of other important aspects of the treatment. An informed consent letter is therefore best understood as the beginning, rather than the end, of a process.*

May 15, 1997

Dear Mr. Edwards,

I provide a letter when I first meet with someone interested in beginning therapy, to explain important aspects of how I work. I encourage you to read it before we meet next, so that you have the chance to ask any questions you have either about my way of working or about psychotherapy in general. Please feel free to bring the letter to our session.

The work I do is best described as psychodynamically-oriented psychotherapy.* Sessions consist of my listening to what a client has to say and then responding with a comment or question. Sometimes I simply remain silent, in order not to interfere with what a client is thinking or feeling. It is natural and expected for very strong feelings to arise during the course of a psychotherapy; coming to understand such feelings is an important part of the work. While not all psychotherapies meet a client's expectations, and a client's symptoms may become more pronounced during the course of therapy, many psychotherapies do help with painful feelings, difficult memories, or conflicts in relating to others. Clients should always feel free during the course of a session to bring up their experience of how the psychotherapy is going.

I hold 45-minute sessions, in my office, at 383 Harvard Street in Cambridge. The frequency of sessions and the length of the psychotherapy are aspects of the work that the client and I decide together. Generally, a psychotherapy will continue until the client and I decide our work is complete. It is important to begin sessions on time; my schedule requires that I end sessions promptly, which means that a client who arrives late for an appointment will not have a full 45-minute session.

Messages for me can be left with my answering service (734-1300) at any time. Although I check my answering service several times each day, I cannot be sure of receiving a message immediately, so that arrangements must be in place should an emergency arise. In an emergency clients may go to the emergency room of any hospital, call 911, or call the Boston Emergency Services Team at 1-800-981-4357. The time to

---

* Some clinicians may want to provide information about their training and background (e.g., Ph.D. or M.D.).

use an emergency room or "911" is when physical safety is at risk.*

My fee is $110 per session. I bill once per month, on the final session of the month. I ask that the bill be paid by the final session of the following month. If more than two months worth of unpaid payments accumulate, it is necessary to discuss and agree upon a payment plan before the psychotherapy can continue.

Clients who use insurance are responsible for co-payments. I encourage clients to read their insurance policies with care; many policies place significant limitations on mental health benefits, and it is important to know what these are. It is also important to know that using mental health benefits may have implications for future insurance coverage. I ask that clients please let me know if it would be helpful to discuss such implications; I am happy to do so.

I do not charge for sessions that are missed because of an emergency or ill health when I have at least 24 hours notice. I do charge for sessions missed with less than 24 hours notice.† Because insurance companies do not cover missed sessions, clients who miss sessions without 24 hours notice are responsible for the full session fee. I ask that clients give at least one week notice of their vacation.

I take approximately four weeks vacation each year. When I am away, another clinician will provide coverage. I will share with the covering clinician any important issues the client and I agree the covering clinician should know about, in case the client needs to contact that person in my absence. The clinician covering for me can be reached through my answering service.

I have both a legal and an ethical duty to ensure that what a client and I talk about remains confidential. In addition, both law and ethics require that I discuss circumstances in which aspects of the work may *not* be kept confidential. First, if I have reason to believe that a child (someone under 18), an elderly person (someone over 60), someone who is disabled, or someone who lives in certain residences, such as a nursing home, is being abused, neglected, or financially exploited, I am legally obligated to disclose this information to a state agency. Laws that are referred to as "mandatory reporting statutes" leave me no room

---

* Therapists who have contracts with managed care companies will need to make sure that nothing in an informed consent letter is inconsistent with their contract. Thus, therapists should be sure to read provisions of the contract that concern availability during emergencies, coverage during vacations, billing, and the like.

† Clinicians who work with individuals struggling with substance abuse may want to explain their policy should a client show up for an appointment under the influence. Some clinicians will treat this circumstance as a session missed without 24 hours notice, which seems perfectly appropriate from a legal, ethical, and clinical point of view.

for discretion; within 24 hours I must convey my concerns to the appropriate authorities. Second, I am obligated to break confidentiality when doing so is necessary to protect an individual's physical safety. Finally, certain legal proceedings would require that information be disclosed. If, for example, a client's mental status, emotional condition, or capacity to care for a child is introduced into a legal proceeding, I may be required to turn records over to a court or to testify. Should a client initiate a legal proceeding that places at issue any aspect of the psychotherapy, the likelihood that confidential information will be disclosed is significantly increased. For clients who would find it helpful, I can provide a copy of the actual laws and regulations governing confidentiality. Should the necessity of releasing confidential information arise, I make every reasonable effort to discuss this matter with the client first; it is my preference to make any such disclosures together with the client, in my office.

I consult with other professionals in the field when I judge that doing so would be helpful to the psychotherapy. When speaking with other professionals I make every reasonable effort to disguise identifying information about a client. Any professional with whom I speak is, like me, bound by confidentiality.

I am not an expert in matters involving the law, and do not conduct evaluations ordered by a court. If a client is involved in, or intends to commence, a legal proceeding in which any aspect of his or her mental or emotional functioning will be examined, it is essential that this matter be discussed as soon as possible.

I am sometimes asked to provide documentation when clients belong to an HMO or are using their insurance. If I receive such a request, it is my policy not to release material until the client and I have discussed the matter.

Finally, it is important to know that other therapies are available. Clients should feel free to explore other therapies if they find this therapy not as helpful as they would like; I can provide referrals to therapists whose way of working is different than my own.

When we next meet I will leave time for you to ask questions you may have about anything in this letter, or about psychotherapy in general.*

I look forward to our next session,

Dr. Elyn Saks

---

* Some clinicians may want to mention the law concerning access to records; whether to do so will, of course, entail a good deal of thinking about the clinical implications of raising this issue. (For a description of the Massachusetts law, see question 102.)

While this letter covers a great deal of material, two points should be emphasized. First, the letter, in and of itself, does not constitute informed consent. Rather, the letter begins a process of discussing with your client the nature, purpose, and intended outcome of the psychotherapy. Second, in regard to a letter, what's most important is not the substance of your policies concerning billing, missed sessions, emergencies, and the like, but rather that you make your policies clear to your client. Adopt whatever policies make most clinical sense to you— but be sure to make those policies clear as you begin your work.

LETTER TERMINATING A THERAPY RELATIONSHIP

In a letter of termination, be sure to state clearly the following: the reasons for termination; your assessment that the treatment is no longer viable; a plan for termination sessions; any conditions that would precipitate a deviation from the plan for termination sessions; a plan for referring the patient to other treaters; and ways in which the patient may obtain treatment on an emergency basis.

Below is an example of a termination letter written by a therapist who has been harassed by a patient. By including each of the elements listed above, the therapist has protected herself from a claim that she abandoned the patient.

Monday, January 27, 1997

Dear Mr. Sheridan,

I am writing this letter to confirm our understanding that our work together will stop as of Monday, February 17. I realize that we discussed the reasons for stopping when we met this afternoon for your weekly session, but I wanted also to write them down in case you had any questions or wanted to review what had been said.

In our first session, we went over how our work together would proceed. My letter of September 17, 1995, in which I outlined our treatment agreement, said that messages could be left with my answering service outside of our regularly scheduled meetings. We also discussed ways to handle emergencies: by calling the Boston Emergency Services Team, going to an emergency room, or calling 911.

This past Fall, beginning in September, you began to call me at night, sometimes as late as 11 P.M. I reminded you that you could leave messages with my answering service outside of our regularly scheduled appointments, and that I did not accept calls at home. You said that you understood and would not call me at home again. In late November, and then around the holidays, I received numerous calls from you. When we met for the first time this year, on January 6, I told you that you must stop calling me at home. While you said that you understood our agreement, and assured me that you would not call me at home again, during the week of January 20 you called me at home no less than 15 times. One call came at 3 A.M. On Friday, January 24, you stopped your car and came to my front door. To the person who answered the door you appeared upset and angry that I was not available to see you. You left only when that person threatened to call the police. I am sorry that you are either unable or unwilling to abide by the agreements we established during our initial sessions.

It has become clear to me that we will no longer be able to work together. For this reason, our work will stop in three weeks. Our regularly scheduled times will be available for termination sessions; these will be on February 3, February 10, and February 17. Our work will stop immediately should you again come to my house or disturb my family.

I am enclosing the names of five clinicians and their phone numbers. I have spoken with the first two, Dr. Ronald Smith and Dr. Judith Barney. Both have said that they have times available in their schedules. In addition, you may seek treatment at the Mental Health Center on Longwood Avenue. I would encourage you to begin contacting possible treaters immediately. I will speak with a treater of your choosing and then send your records to that individual as soon as you sign a release for me to do so. Also, as we have discussed numerous times, and as I explained in my September 1995 letter to you, emergency treatment is available at any hospital emergency room, by calling 911, or by calling the Boston Emergency Services Team at 1-800-981-4357.

If you have any questions, please bring this letter with you to our February 3 session so that we may discuss them.

I will see you on February 3, and hope that our session can focus on how to make this transition go as smoothly as possible for you.

Sincerely,

Dr. Elyn Saks

BIBLIOGRAPHY

Appelbaum, P. S., & Gutheil, T. G. (1991). *Clinical handbook of psychiatry and the law* (2nd ed.). Baltimore: Williams & Wilkins.

Appelbaum, P. S., & Roth, L. H. (1981). Clinical issues in the assessment of competency. *American Journal of Psychiatry,* 138, 1462–1467.

Appelbaum, P. S., Lidz, C. W., & Meisel, A. (1987). *Informed consent: Legal theory and clinical practice.* New York: Oxford University.

American Psychiatric Association. (1994). *Diagnostic and statistical manual of mental disorders* (4th ed.). Washington, D.C.: Author.

American Psychiatric Association. (1995). *The principles of medical ethics, with annotations especially applicable to psychiatry.* Washington, D.C.: Author.

American Psychological Association. (1992, December). Ethical principles of psychologists and code of conduct. *American Psychologist,* pp. 1597–1611.

American Psychological Association Ethics Committee. (1992, December). Rules and procedures. *American Psychologist,* pp. 1612–1628.

Bray, J. H., Shepherd, J. N., & Hays, J. R. (1985). Legal and ethical issues in informed consent to psychotherapy. *The American Journal of Family Therapy,* 13, 50–60.

Berkowitz, S. (1979–1996). Legal briefing [column]. *Massachusetts Psychological Association Quarterly.*

Brant, J. (1991). *Law and mental health professionals: Massachusetts.* Washington, D.C.: American Psychological Association.

Clark, D. C., & Fawcett, J. (1992). An empiracally based model of suicide risk assessment for patients with affective disorder. In D. Jacobs, *Suicide and clinical practice* (pp. 55–73). Washington, D.C.: American Psychiatric Press.

Clark, D. C., & Fawcett, J. (1992). Review of empirical risk factors for evaluation of the suicidal patient. In B. Bongar, *Suicide: Guidelines for assessment, management, and treatment* (pp. 16–48). New York: Oxford.

Furlong, E. D. (1995). Coercion in the community: The application of Rogers guardianship to outpatient commitment. *New England Journal on Criminal and Civil Confinement,* 21, 485–508.

Gabbard, G., & Lester, E. (1996). *Boundaries and boundary violations.* New York: Basic.

Grisso, T. (1986). *Evaluating competencies: Forensic assessment and instruments.* New York: Plenum.

Handelsman, M. M., & Galvin, M. D. (1988). Facilitating informed consent for outpatient psychotherapy: A suggested written format. *Professional Psychology: Research and Practice,* 19, 223–225.

Handelsman, M. M., Kemper, M. B., Kesson-Craig, P., McLain, J., & Johnsrud, C. (1986). Use, content, and readability of written informed consent forms for treatment. *Professional Psychology: Research and Practice,* 17, 514–518.

Katz, J. (1984). *The silent world of doctor and patient.* New York: Free.

Keith-Speigel, P., & Koocher, G. P. (1985). *Ethics in psychology. Professional standards and cases.* New York: Random House.

Millstein, B., Rubenstein, L., & Cyr, R. (1991, March). The Americans with Disabilities Act: A breathtaking promise for people with mental disabilities. *Clearinghouse Review,* pp. 1240–1249.

Nolan, J. R., Nolan-Haley, J. M., Connolly, M. J., Hicks, S. C., & Albrandi, M. N. (1990). *Black's law dictionary: Definition of the terms and phrases of American and English jurisprudence, ancient and modern* (6th ed). St. Paul: West.

McBeth, J. E., Wheeler, A. M., Sither, J. W., Onek, J. N. (1994). *Legal and risk management issues in the practice of psychiatry.* Washington, D.C.: Psychiatrists' Purchasing Group.

Physicians' desk reference. (1997). Montvale, NJ: Medical Economics.

Rozovsky, F. A. (1990). *Consent to treatment* (2nd ed.). Boston: Little, Brown.

Supreme Judicial Court of Massachusetts. (1989). *Report of the gender bias study of the Supreme Judicial Court.* Boston: Author.

Tribe, L. H. (1988). *American constitutional law* (2nd ed.). Mineola, N.Y.: Foundation.

Winslade, W. J., & Ross, J. W. (1983). *The insanity plea.* New York: Charles Scribner's Sons.

Woodward, B., Duckworth, K. S., & Gutheil, T. G. (1983). Pharmacotherapist-psychotherapist collaboration. In J. M. Oldham, M. B., Riba, & A. Tasman, *American Psychiatric Press review of psychiatry* (pp. 631–649). Washington, D.C.: American Psychiatric Press.

INDEX

INDEX OF CASES

INDEX OF STATUTES

* Massachusetts General Law

INDEX OF REGULATIONS

INDEX OF SUBJECTS

† Code of Massachusetts Regulation